"This book is the one book that I will treasure for the rest of my Eric Mann has written a book that is timeless, and I congratulate him for a job well done.
I am looking forward to reading his next book, anxiously."

- K.A. Schwartz

"I loved this book - I could not put it down. At many moments, I literally laughed out loud. I think that anyone who grew up in the 60s and 70s from any neighborhood in any town could enjoy this book. It was about a time when kids actually played outside, and made lasting memories."

- M. Brown

"The author is a great storyteller, bringing each person and event to life, making you long to be a kid during that era again. Hysterical, uplifting, and truly laugh-out-loud funny!"

- A.R. Eichem

"It evokes the simplicity of the times, and of the sweet and wonderful "Leave it to Beaver" town that nurtured us. It evokes happy memories, sentiment, and laughter, much like the "Mann" who wrote it."

- Thaenil Mrakus

The Delmont Street Gang

By

Eric A. Mann

The Delmont Street Gang, Copyright © 2012
by Eric A. Mann. All rights reserved.
No part of this book may be used or reproduced in any manner whatsoever without written permission.

Cover Art by Amy Ahrendt-Strocchia

Dedication

I lovingly dedicate this book, such as it is, to the friends of my youth, who I'll never be able to replace, who I'll never forget. I hope that you like what I've done here, and don't seek revenge.

Acknowledgements

Thanks to my wife, Susan Kearns-Mann, for her love, tolerance and friendship for more than thirty years. The fact that I can still make you laugh tells me that I haven't worn out my welcome.

Thanks to Irv and Marilyn Mann, my dad and mom, for giving me a sense of humor, a self-worth, and the courage to speak my mind, for better or for worse. I miss you both, every day.

Foreword

Why am I writing this book, and who's going to care? Ah dunno!

I've had a habit of regaling (ad nauseum) my friends, acquaintances and co-workers with stories and anecdotes from my life, and the lives of my family and friends, which were passed onto me throughout the years. Many times, I have heard someone say "You should write these down – they would make a great book!" I never took them seriously. I mean, you see stories like these made into books, movies and television shows, so someone must be paying attention!

I have my favorites, too – stories that made me feel good; stories that made me reminisce about my own youth – "Stand By Me", "The Wonder Years", "The Sandlot", just to name a few. I can, and will read or watch these stories anytime I have the chance, because they tell of a time that was easier to comprehend, easier to live. We were kids! And, what the hell did _we_ know about real troubles? That was our parents' job to worry about those things. Our job was to go to school, do our homework, obey our parents, and have fun. That was it, in a nutshell.

To that end, I share these stories with you – the types of stories that old friends share at a reunion, usually predicated by *"remember the time ...?"* - The types of stories that my wife usually rolls her eyes at, because I'm telling that old story again. Some are about certain fond memories that may not have a plot, as much as they are a part of the overall fabric of a kid's life in a small town. They may not be in chronological order, but does that matter?

I hope you have your own stories, and I hope this book motivates you to write them down, if for nothing else than to share with your family and friends.

Don't let your stories be lost.

And remember, the following is all true. The names were changed to protect the morons.

Chapter One
The Delmont Street Gang

Growing up in the sixties and early seventies in a town like Manchester, Connecticut, was like one huge playground. It was truly, as the town motto read, the "City of Village Charm". You knew all of your neighbors, and cared about them. The streets were tree-lined; the houses neat and well-kept. Kids walked to school by themselves, and stayed after school for scouts or other extra-curricular activities, then walked home.

The stores were family-owned and operated, and the owners were friends of the community. It was as if your parents knew them all on a first-name basis. Everyone burned leaves in the fall, shoveled walks in the winter, and sweltered in the summer – nobody had home air conditioning, back then.

It was Memorial Day Parades, July Fourth fireworks, Labor Day at the beach, high school football, county fairs, concerts in the park, and caroling at Christmas. It was milk in glass bottles and baked goods delivered to your home. It was a parking lot full of hot rods and muscle cars, parked at McDonald's, on a Friday night. Family dinners took place every night, and every member of the family was expected to be present.

Gas was cheap. Going to the movies was an exciting event, soda bottles were returned for deposit, a pack of baseball cards was a nickel, the local news broadcast followed Santa's progress on Christmas Eve, and when the Good Humor Ice Cream truck came into your neighborhood, you lost your mind!

It's been said that "It takes an entire village to raise a child". Well, this was no more prevalent than in my neighborhood. If you were seen causing trouble, not only would you "get it" by the adult who caught you, but you would "get it" even worse, when you got home. AND, if one of you got in trouble, ALL of you got in trouble – you were guilty by association.

There was no cable television, just three channels. There were no video games, no DVD's, no scheduled play dates. Just neighborhood after neighborhood of kids of all ages who heard the same daily demand from their parents: *"Go outside and play!"*

I don't know if our neighborhood demographics were typical for the era, but in our immediate square block, the kids' population was comprised of thirty boys and fourteen girls. I lived on Summit Street, with my parents, Irv and Marilyn, and my sisters, Jessica and Claudia. I was the only son, middle child. We were one of a very few white-collar, upper-middle class families living in a blue collar neighborhood. My parents told me that they moved there so that my sisters and I would be exposed to people from all walks of life. I used to think they did it so I would get the shit kicked out of me on a regular basis.

I was a dork! Plain and simple! I was a foot taller than most of my friends, and grew so fast that I was this clumsy kid, trying to grow into this oversized body. Hell, I was six feet tall, at twelve! Add a pair of crooked, tortoise-shell horn-rimmed glasses, a crew cut, and an overly loud mouth, and I was quite a catch! I look back at those yearly pictures that we used to get taken at school, and I looked like I ought to be riding on the short bus.

I didn't always fit in. I remember feeling like I didn't belong, and that I was doomed to be the brunt of everyone's jokes and taunting. There were times that I didn't even want to go to grade school, because of the teasing. I don't know why kids are like that. Someone's always looking to make himself feel better by destroying someone else. But, I guess if I asked my classmates, many of them would feel the same way. I guess it's a part of growing up, sad as that is.

My parents were well-educated and extremely artistic, and painstakingly exposed their kids to books, museums, music, theater and art - all the key areas that, if brought up in front of your friends, usually warranted a response of *"What a WUSS!"*

But, the arts had an impact on me; most notably music. It actually changed my life. Specifically, February 9, 1964 – the night the Beatles first appeared on the Ed Sullivan Show. I was exactly eight days shy of my seventh birthday. This was new! This was exciting! I turned to my parents, and said "I wanna play drums, like Ringo!" I would end up taking lessons for seven years.

I tell you all this, because this was mine. No matter what the other kids could do, or excel at, this was where I fit in – music. It helped my confidence, and improved my coordination, so that I wasn't falling over my own feet. To this day, the arts are a part of my life. Thanks Mom and Dad!

More on music, later...

Around the corner from our house was a dead end street (in today's lingo, this is called a cul de sac – big f-ing deal!) where the majority of us congregated. This was Delmont Street. At any given time several of us might be playing wiffle ball, street football, or some other game. There were, virtually, no fences, and people didn't seem to care if kids were running through their back yards during a game of "Hide-n-Seek", "Five, Ten, One of my Men" or, my favorite version, "Chase Game". On summer evenings, the kids would be outside to well after dark, while the parents would visit with each other on their front porches. Many nights, I can remember playing outside till after ten o'clock. Then, after we were good and tired, the moms would call us in, and we would pass out for the night.

As in most neighborhoods, there was a definite pecking order among the boys. Somehow, along the way, we were broken up into two groups: the "Big Kids" and the

"Little Kids". I can only assume that some of the older kids came up with this distinction based solely upon one's age group. A few months either way could mean the world to your status in the neighborhood. This concept was always a source of frustration to me, as I was considered a "Little Kid" because I was a year younger than the youngest "Big Kid". It didn't matter that I was twice the size of their youngest, or that I was stronger; their "Leader" made the call, and that was tantamount to one of the Ten Commandments: "So it is written, so it shall be done."

This leader I speak of? Craig Haley. He was the oldest of six kids, and just about the toughest, most intimidating big kid in the neighborhood. He was also a tremendous bully, never hesitating to haul off and smack some other kid, because he thought the kid deserved it. I remember asking him: "Craig, when will I be considered a 'Big Kid'?" With a sneer on his lips, he took great joy in responding with one word: "Never!" The leader had spoken.

A short list of the other big kids – Ricky Hirsch, Steve and Rod McNulty, Steve and Burl Carter, Bob Dora, Freddy Corrado, Mickey Callahan and Burt Stewart.

Throughout the years, there were many arguments and fistfights among the boys. It seemed that never a week would pass without someone "duking it out" or being pissed off at someone else. You put that much adolescent testosterone in the same area, and explosions are likely to take place. The funny thing about these fights, they were usually over in a couple of hits, someone would give up and by the following day, the disagreement was forgotten. I think we all realized that we <u>had</u> to let go of any animosity because, good or bad, we depended upon each other for our daily activities. You alienate yourself from the rest of the kids, and you could blow the entire summer vacation.

For the most part, I hung around with a select group of the "Little Kids": Larry and Karl Smith, Ryan and Matt Haley, Ted and Ken Hanson, Sid Orlowski and David Corrado. Various other "Little Kids" were in and out of our circle, but this was the main nucleus.

Larry and Karl were unique, as they, along with their little brother, Reese, were the sons of the only divorced couple any of us ever knew, while we were growing up. This was tantamount to scandal, back then. Their divorced mother was Donna Smith, a highly-stressed

Italian woman, who was saddled with the job of raising three small boys on her own. For years, my family shared the holidays with the Smiths – Christmas at one house, Thanksgiving at the other...

Larry, the oldest, was one of the more intelligent guys in the neighborhood. He possessed a dry, warped sense of humor, who was a master of delivering quality, not quantity with his jokes. He was always good for an intelligent conversation, if that was possible among a bunch of adolescent pinheads like us.

Karl was just plain funny. He was able to crack us up at a moment's notice. Whether it was a smartass comment, or a well-placed fart, Karl was funny. I remember the two of us at the same house party, and Karl sitting in the kitchen, flipping slices of American cheese against the ceiling, where they would stick. Why? Because he could. Days later, cheese slices were still mysteriously falling from the sky. One time, we were in his family den, watching TV, when the broadcast had technical difficulties. The lettering on the screen read "Please Stand By". Without missing a beat, we both jumped up, and stood by the television, and laughed like a couple of idiots, amazed that we both had the same idea. I guess you had to be there...

Larry and Karl had a great knack for "pushing their mom's buttons" by making some smartass comment and getting her really riled up. It was a regular occurrence to see this little, wiry Italian woman transform into her "fighter plane pose", as she was yelling at the boys – both arms straight back behind her, neck craning forward, lips stretched open revealing her clenched teeth – she looked like a P-51 Mustang!

The Smith boys and I played in the same Junior Alumni Baseball League. One evening, Mrs. Smith was giving the three of us a ride to practice. When her car pulled up in front of my house, Karl was in the front passenger seat, and Larry was in the back seat, seated behind his mom. I climbed into the back seat, next to Larry, and noticed an immediate tension. Karl and his mom were in the midst of an argument. Larry flashed me a nervous grin, which told me that this was going to be good.

I don't remember what the argument was about; I just remember that the content was typical of what was heard on any given day in our neighborhood between one of the guys and a parent – usually the mom (with Dad, there was always a chance you would get your ass kicked...) demanding that her son act like a human being, and the son firing back with a series of wise-guy retorts, causing the mom to lose her mind, and chase the son around the house, in an attempt to snuff out his short, disrespectful life.

Anyway, Mrs. Smith was railing on about Karl's "attitude", and Karl was firing back. Of course, the barrage would become escalated, as Karl now had an audience, with me in the car. For the next two miles across town, I had my face buried in my baseball glove, as my entire body convulsed as I vainly tried to stifle my laughter. You never wanted to embarrass the parents by letting them know you were laughing at their frustration. That was another can of worms no kid wanted to open!

When the verbal exchange reached its pinnacle, Mrs. Smith delivered an ultimatum:

> *"Karl, if you don't knock it off right now, I'm going to wrap this car around a pole!"*

Whereby LARRY, not Karl – LARRY who had been all but silent during the entire ride chimed in:

> "There's a nice elm tree over there!"

I lost it. Involuntarily, I let out a huge "puh-HAH-HAH-HAH-HAHHHHHH!" By the time I had regained my composure, Mrs. Smith had pulled the car over to the side of the road, and brought it to an abrupt halt. Then, she started giving it to me, with both barrels:

> "Eric, you think it's FUNNY the way they treat their mother?"
>
> "Well, no, I..."
>
> "You find humor in their lack of respect for me?"
>
> "I didn't mean to..."
>
> "Get out of my car!"
>
> "But, we're two miles from..."
>
> "Get OUT!"

I BLEW it! I broke the Cardinal Rule. You NEVER let the parents know that the kids think they're a bunch of fools who have no idea what's going on! I was now, and forever, on Mrs. Smith's Shit List. Sheepishly, I opened the car door, and slowly swung one leg out, and then the other; all the time hoping she'd have a change of heart – she didn't care that I was more than two miles from home, and I would have to walk.

As I closed the car door, and the car started to pull away, Karl leaned out the window, and shouted: "Remember, just keep on laughing!"

Ryan and Matt were two of six kids in the Haley family. Ryan was a total maniac with a bicycle (and, anything else, for that matter), reckless beyond belief. It was as if nobody ever told him that he could get killed. He held the Delmont Street record for the longest "wheelie", and used to think it was cool to ride around with no tire on his rear bike wheel, because of the "neat" sparks it would make. Ryan was also a major scam artist. He would think nothing of stealing ten dollars out of his mother's purse, dropping the bill in a bush down the street then, picking one of us to take a walk by that same bush, miraculously finding the money, and believing he had an airtight alibi. His mother was never fooled.

One time, his mom had grounded him, and sent him to his room. Then, she sat in the living room, at the bottom of the stairs, to make sure Ryan didn't try to sneak out.

Ryan refused to take his punishment lying down, and started working on Mrs. Haley's sanity, hoping he would wear her down:

"Mom! Can I go out and play?"

"No!"

"Mom! Can I go out and play?"

"No!"

"Mom! Can I go out and play?"

"No!"

"Mom! Can I go out and play?"

"If you open your mouth one more time, I'm gonna kill you, and make it look like an accident!"

Well, that didn't work. So, Ryan did what any self-respecting con-man would do – he tied a string to a building block, lowered it out his bedroom window, and used it to knock on the back door. When Mrs. Haley went to answer it, Ryan ran down the stairs, and out the front door. It's a good thing he never took up a life of crime, because no prison could hold him.

Matt was hilarious. Although he was about three years younger than the rest of us, he was accepted. He would do anything to make us laugh. *"Matt! Eat this bug!", "Matt! Drink this!", "Matt! Put this bag of flaming dog shit on that front porch...!"* I remember Mrs. Haley, traditionally getting frustrated with Matt's antics, and yelling *"Matt! Stop acting like a mental!"* Ahh, the joys of parenting!

One time, while all of us were together one evening, Matt allowed six of us to pick him up, and pretend to bang him into a stop sign, head first, while he screamed "bloody murder". Eventually, some well-meaning passerby would pull up in their car, and jump out to rescue Matt from the feigned brutality. We would then drop Matt on the adjacent grass, and take off running, leaving Matt to roll around, screaming in mock pain, trying not to laugh out loud, as the Good Samaritan would chase us down the street. When the "rescuer" was far enough away, Matt would hop to his feet, throw out his best "HA, HA!", and run away. We always imagined our victims standing there, turning into a huge candy "sucker", as they always did in the Warner Brothers cartoons.

Teddy Hanson moved to town during our Second Grade year of school. We met because I helped him pick out his desk, from the supply in the Bentley School basement. He was one of the most naturally-gifted athletes I have ever seen. He could play any position on a baseball team, and be the best. He could also play basketball better than anyone in the neighborhood. I envied that.

Teddy was also a bit of a bully. But, unlike Craig Haley, Teddy would always work his way back into our good graces, regardless of what torture he inflicted upon the members of our group. He and I were forever getting into tangles, either verbal or physical. Yet, I always forgave him. I don't know why, either. It might have been the fact that we were both huge Red Sox fans – which was a big deal, because, in our neighborhood, you were a Red Sox or Yankees fan, and dependent upon the company you kept, you could end up with a punch in the eye!

Teddy lived with his parents, Ted senior and Florence, and four siblings – Ken, Pam, George and Irene. Teddy's brothers and sisters looked up to him. Why not? They were scared to death of him – do what he says, or suffer his wrath.

David Corrado was probably my best friend growing up. He was one of four kids born to Bob and Diane Corrado. He had an older sister, Teri, an older brother Freddy, and a younger sister, Mindy. Mr. Corrado was a strict Italian father who never let loose his grip on the kids. When everyone else was playing outside after dark on a summer night, acting like idiots, the Corrados had to be in the house, in bed.

Because David was in bed so early, he would show up at seven o'clock every morning and stand under my bedroom window, shouting: "Errrrrrric, come out and play!" My mom would yell: "Will you tell David to knock it off? People are trying to sleep!"

The earliest memory that I have of hanging out with David, is when we were about four or five, and our moms were having coffee in the Corrados' kitchen, while we tore up the backyard. David and I decided to try to carry a cast iron fireplace grate across the yard, and David let go and dropped it on my big toe, taking the toenail clean off. What a pal!

Another time, David and I were in the Smith's front yard, which was the drop-off point for our newspaper bundles (Larry, Karl, Teddy, David and I all delivered…). We were messing around with the rest of the guys when, for some twisted reason I have never figured out, David threw a leaf rake at me, while yelling "Think fast!" – It hit me right in the face! Hurt like hell! As I shook out the cobwebs, I saw David running home, afraid he was going to get his ass kicked up around his ears.

So, I retaliated the only way I could – I carried his bicycle half way up a telephone pole, and hung it there, where it remained for two days. That is, until his father made me take it down. Good times, good times.

Sid Orlowski was one of eleven kids born to Stan and Bonnie Orlowski. They actually lived on Hollister Street, directly across from Bentley Elementary School. They lived in a huge Victorian house, and ate their meals in shifts. And, if eleven kids wasn't enough chaos, they also owned a rhesus monkey, who the kids in the neighborhood loved. And, do you wanna know something interesting? Monkeys really do fling their own shit!

The Orlowskis used to buy the biggest tubs of peanut butter and jelly I had ever seen. They were the only family in our "gang" who had a laundry chute. I remember a never-ending pile of laundry in the basement. I mean, with 13 people adding to the pile, who could keep up? They also owned a cottage on Coventry Lake, in the next town over. It was a treat when you were lucky enough to be invited up to the cottage, for the day. They were the only family we knew who owned a speed boat. They were also the first family with a color console television. These were just two of the many prizes Mrs. Orlowski had won on a nationally-televised game show, called "Charge Account", with Jan Murray, as the host.

Anyway, I remember them inviting several of the kids in the neighborhood over to the house to see <u>The Wizard of Oz</u> in color. All we knew was black and white.

The other thing for which I'll always remember Sid was the time he peeled a huge scab (and, I'm talking four to five inches) off of his elbow, while in school, didn't know what to do with it, so put it in his shirt pocket, and brought it home! Now, THAT'S an interesting anecdote!

These were the guys that I ran with. The ones I spent every waking moment with – The ones who mattered in my short life.

Chapter Two
Insanity Runs in the Family

My mom and dad, Marilyn and Irv, were the favorite parents in the neighborhood. You know, where one of your friends would say *"Boy, I wish your parents were my parents!",* and you look at them as if they'd lost their freaking mind. Your own parents were never as cool as your friend's. Although, come to think of it, I never DID think the other parents were very cool...

My parents were responsible for taking the neighborhood kids on many of the outings they still remember as adults. It was not uncommon for my dad to load the station wagon with kids and travel the hour and a half ride to the Rhode Island beaches, or to the amusement park. None of the other parents did that.

Dad was my hero; as much grief as I caused him, I always looked up to him. No matter what kind of day he had, Dad was always glad to get home to his family. He always greeted me with a smile on his face. We would play catch in the backyard or swim in the pool, or watch a ball game together.

Dad was "Old School" – a depression-era kid, who grew up on the South side of Chicago. One of his neighborhood buddies was Al Capone's illegitimate son. Dad used to tell of how Capone would come to the neighborhood to visit. The gangster would step out of his car, take out a couple of rolls of quarters, crush them up in his bare hands, and throw them up in the air, laughing like crazy while the kids clamored for their new-found fortune. Hey! That was big money back then!

He was a veteran of World War II, and later attended DePaul University, where he met my mom. They dated, married, and had three kids – Jessica, in 1953, Me, in 1957, and Claudia, in 1959.

He moved the family to Manchester, Connecticut in 1959, where he started working as an engineer for Pratt and Whitney Aircraft. Over the years, there would be several engineering jobs for several companies, in several towns – too many to list here.

Dad was a creature of habit. Case in point, whenever we would pile in the car to go wherever, we would routinely keep our collective mouths shut, just to see where Dad would lead us. More times than not, we would end up at the Manchester Parkade, our local shopping mall. Dad would pull the car into the parking lot, and we would bust up laughing. He'd get so pissed!

"Why didn't someone tell me?"

"We wanted to see if you'd figure it out!"

"Goddammit!"

He was also a typical male, in that he refused to ask anyone for directions. One time while on vacation in Cape Cod, we were in the car, doing some sightseeing, when we ended up getting lost. Well, despite my mother's insistence, dad refused to stop and ask for help. He took a turn onto a main street, and we found ourselves stuck in the middle of a Fourth of July parade, unable to exit, due to the police barricades. We were appalled. Mom's yelling at Dad, Dad's yelling back at Mom, Jessie's hiding under the back seat out of total shame, and thousands of vacationers were asking each other "Who the heck are <u>those</u> people, and why are they in our parade???"

My mom was nuts! I say that in the most loving way, but the truth remains. She had a tremendously quick wit, and could zing you with a one-liner before you knew what hit you. I guess that's where I get it. She was also known for her "colorful" language, to go along with her high-pitched yell: "JEE-zus CHRIST! Knock that SHIT OFF!!!" or "You smartass little bastard!" We could never take these tirades personally. We were too busy laughing. One time I thought she was going to kill me, when she called me a *"little son-of-a-bitch"* and I replied *"Well, you would be the judge of that!"* Never ran so fast in my life.

Mom was the disciplinarian in the household. One or more of us would be acting up and, after repeated requests for us to act like human beings, the top of her head would pop off from the pressure, and she would spin on her heels, march into the living room, where my dad was usually reading the paper, and say "Ir-VING, give me your belt!" And the race was on!

Truth be told, she was funny as hell! She did things that I NEVER saw another mom do. Case in point:

For years, Mom and Dad belonged to a local theater group, called Little Theater of Manchester. This group was known for producing high quality plays, and had quite a reputation throughout the Northeast. One time, the group was producing Toby Tyler, a play about a boy who runs away to join a circus. One of the main characters was a "dancing bear", which required one of the actors to perform in a bear costume. Well, Mom was not about to let this opportunity to go by. She decided to have a little fun, and took the costume home.

Back in the sixties, there were certain individuals that every family knew, such as the mailman. Our mailman was named Charlie, and every day you could hear him coming down the street, whistling all the way, waving hello to the neighbors; truly loving his job. Every day Charlie would turn up the sidewalk leading up to our house, bound up the three cement steps, slap open the lid of our painted steel mailbox, toss the mail in, slap the lid down, and head on to the next house. This was the daily routine…except for this day.

Charlie turned up our sidewalk, bound up the three cement steps, slapped open the lid of our mailbox, tossed the mail in, slapped the lid down, and Mom, dressed in the bear costume, flung open the front door, and let out a huge roar! Charlie's face turned white, as he stumbled backwards down the steps, giving Mom untold enjoyment. When Charlie got his composure, and realized that he hadn't soiled himself, he and Mom had a good laugh.

Mom then talked Dad into dressing up in the costume, and allowing her to walk him around the neighborhood, as kids were running into their houses, yelling "The Manns bought a bear, the Manns bought a bear!"

About a year later, the theater group was producing Androcles and the Lion which, of course, required an actor to dress in a lion's costume. Here comes Charlie to deliver the day's mail, bounds up the three steps, slaps open the lid of the mailbox, the front door opens, and one paw emerges to receive the mail. Charlie, without missing a beat, said *"I was expecting this."*

I thought that both of my sisters, Jessica and Claudia, were huge pains in my ass! Jessie is three years older, and Claudia is two years younger than me. There was just enough age difference between us that we had nothing in common with each other. By the time we were teenagers, we all had different groups of friends and different interests, and only saw each other at family meals, outings or national holidays. We were, for all intents and purposes, strangers in the same house.

Jessie barely tolerated me. I was the annoying little turd, who was constantly encroaching upon her personal space. The day my mom brought me home from the hospital, and introduced Jessy to her new little brother, she protested: *"I don't WANT a little brother! I want a PUPPY!"* Thus, our future relationship was firmly established.

I called Jess the "Independent Dependent", which cracked my parents up! In one breath, she would defiantly announce "I don't need anybody!", and in the second breath ask our dad for money for records.

When Jessie was around twelve, she was old enough to babysit Claudia and me. And, she made the most of it, by blackmailing us to do her bidding:

> *"Go get me a bowl of ice cream!"*
>
> *"No!"*

> *"Fine! Then I'll tell Mom that you were bad, and you'll be in TROUBLE!"*
>
> *"Okay! Okay! Don't tell Mom!"*

Jessie loved to make me look like an idiot. And, I made her dreams come true on many occasions. More than once, I can remember her giving me cocktail onions, and telling me they were grapes. And, of course, I would pop them in my mouth, gag, then start crying, as Jess would laugh like a sadistic minion from Hell.

Claudia was my version of Lisa Simpson. She was the book reader, the thinker, the nerd, who was my playmate, when the guys weren't around. She was the one I built forts with in the basement, rode skateboards with, or played board games. She also put up with a lot of my crap. Truth be told, I probably wasn't very nice to her. I think I was probably jealous of her hogging my parents' affection. Funny… come to think of it… that's probably what Jessie was pissed off about.

Claudia had allergies – lots and lots of allergies, and, asthma. Her childhood was spent in and out of the hospital. Not a lot of fun. However, I sometimes thought that she used her ailment to her advantage. For instance, a bunch of us would be playing tag in the schoolyard, and every time someone would be ready to tag her, Claudia would say "Time out! I'm having trouble breathing!" Her pursuer would tire of waiting for Claudia to feel better, and take off to chase someone else. Like a miracle, she would recover and rejoin the game, moments later. Pretty slick!

In retrospect, she was probably telling the truth.

Chapter Three

There Are Heroes, And Then There Are Heroes

I remember going to Fenway Park with my dad. As we lived in Connecticut, it was about 1 1/2 hours to the park, and the anticipation grew as we traveled up the Mass Pike.

We would always go fairly early, usually getting there at about 11:00 AM for a day game, so that we could see batting practice and, hopefully, I could get one of the players to look over my way, for a photo, or an autograph, whatever.

We used to park on the street, 3 or 4 blocks from Yawkey Way, and walk over. The street vendors would be setting up shop for the day, and my heart would pump faster, as we got close to the entry gates, and that famed brick facade, with the red-lettered sign, reading Fenway Park.

When we were allowed to enter, I immediately noticed the musty smell of spilled beer, and steaming Fenway

Franks, to go along with the sound of vendors yelling "Hey! Programs heah! Gitchyah programs heah!" We would follow the signs directing us to the first base seats, and turn into the tunnel, turn into the light. As I would walk up the ramp, the anticipation swelling, this monument would rise up in front of me; this wall of legend; this Green Monster.

I would always stop at the top of the ramp, to take it all in - the green, green grass, the sky so blue, it would hurt your eyes, the rich, perfect infield dirt, the crisp, white uniforms of my favorite team, the pock marked hand rails scraped and painted year after year with the same glossy paint, and the kids all squished up against the retaining wall, begging for autographs, balls, whatever.

My dad always arranged to get seats right behind the Red Sox dugout. Several times, we would be in the first row, leaning right on it. That was the best, because I knew that my team was sitting right in front of me. I, like a thousand other hopeful kids, would bring my baseball glove, in hopes of catching that elusive foul ball. I never did.

It was game time - the starting lineups would be announced, the Sox would take the field, and the National Anthem would be sung. It was time for baseball; it was time for my heroes.

Dad would show me how to fill in my scorecard, explain what "LOB" meant, predict the next pitch, cheer with me, groan with me and, most importantly, be there with me. A shared laugh, a shared frustration, a shared day. It was the best.

Although the Sox didn't always win, I did. For, truth be told, my beloved Sox aside, my real hero was my dad, and these lifelong memories he made for me.

Chapter Four

Autograph Day

It was the Summer of '69. I was twelve. My dad and I had made the hour and a half drive from Connecticut to Fenway, to take in a Sunday afternoon game. Like I said, we usually arrived at the park at eleven, in order to watch batting practice.

But, this would be a special day. The Sox were starting a brand-new promotion, where two of our beloved Red Sox would be signing autographs for one hour before the game. And, I was fourth in line.

Who would it be? To whom would I have a fleeting chance to mumble and stutter a few words, in hopes of impressing these big leaguers with my vast baseball knowledge? Would it be some mop-up pitcher out of the bullpen? Some rarely used utility infielder? It didn't matter. We were getting the chance to meet someone who actually wore that uniform for a living; someone who had made it; someone we all wanted to be.

I looked behind me, and the line was snaking down one aisle, and up into the cheap seats on the first base side. The anticipation was building, and the kids were murmuring to each other, almost afraid to speak above a whisper, for fear that we'd be asked to leave the line for being disruptive.

It was time. Out from the dugout walked our first guest signer. It was Bob Montgomery, our starting catcher! Well, this was cool! Bob was on the field every day; a major player. He sat behind a table, which had been set up on the dirt, adjacent to the dugout, and waited.

Then, it happened. I heard one of the kids in front exclaim in a hushed voice: "Oh my God!"

Rising out of the dugout, with his hat pulled low over his forehead, his bright white uniform almost glowing under the sun, a commanding presence - a god to me, and every other kid in that line - the "Great Number Eight", the "Captain", my hero, Carl Yastrzemski!

I couldn't breathe. There he was, sitting just feet away! I was going to meet the man! I was going to have my touch with greatness! What would I say? What COULD I say? Just keep cool! Just keep cool!

Finally, one of the ushers pulled back the gate leading to the field, and let the first two kids approach the table. Yaz and Monty were signing stacks of eight-by-ten photos, and handing them to each kind. It was an assembly line. It had to be.

I didn't care. It was my turn. I sheepishly approached the table, and my hero passed me a photo, while he continued to sign his stack of glossies. But, I paused for a second, and said "Thank you, Mister Yastrzemski." Yaz stopped writing, mid-autograph, as if I had said something foreign, something unexpected. He slowly looked up at me, his eyes squinting from the sun, smiled a half-smile, and simply said "You're welcome".

It was over. I was shuffled away by the usher. I walked back to my seat behind the dugout, cherishing my prized possession, cherishing my moment with Yaz. I showed my dad the photo, and he chucked me on the shoulder, and told me that I would remember this day for the rest of my life.

I sat there for the rest of the hour, looking over at Yaz, as he handed out photo after photo, thinking my moment with him was better than anyone else's that day. He actually spoke to me. We had a connection.

That was over forty years ago. I'm looking up at the bookcase in my office, and there's the photo. I had it mounted on a trophy board, with an engraved plaque, which reads:

Carl Yastrzemski

Triple Crown 1967

3000 Hit Club

HOF 1989

I think about that day, and I still get emotional. For, Yaz fulfilled a dream for this twelve-year-old. I was just a face in the crowd to Yaz, that day, but he gave me a memory which will remain with me for the rest of my life.

Chapter Five
Nicknames and Aliases

Several of the guys ended up with nicknames, bestowed upon them by someone else in the group, typically for one of three reasons:

- A term of endearment – very rare
- To make fun of a personal affliction – somewhat common
- To make fun of the guy's name – very common

Not everyone had a nickname – not everyone wanted one. But, the fact was, once one took hold, you rarely got rid of it, without an act of congress.

Some of the more memorable nicknames in our neighborhood:

"Shit Stain" – Given to Larry Smith. He had a favorite blue, woolen stocking cap, with a red stripe around the bottom. Apparently the cap had been left on a hot radiator in his house, leaving a brown burn mark on it.

His brother, Karl, took one look at it, and said "It looks like a shit stain!"

"Nope! It's a burn mark!"

"Shit Stain!"

"Burn mark!"

"Shit Stain!'

"Shut up!"

"Make me!"

(SMACK!)

You know, Larry wore that hat for years! He probably still has it!

"Face" – Given to Reese Smith <u>and</u> George Hanson by their respective older brothers, it was supposed to be a commentary on their ugly mugs. Funny thing was, I don't remember either of them as ugly. I believe it to be more a case of sibling bullying.

"Grinley" – David Corrado. I believe Teddy hung this on him. He had a big grin, and it seemed to fit. It was eventually shortened to "Grin".

"Tippy" – Ricky Hirsch; one of the "Big Kids". He used to walk with a bounce in his step, on his tippy-toes. He reminded everyone of a cartoon character, and was always dirty – like Pig Pen, in the "Peanuts" comic strips. One time, a bunch of the guys, led by Craig Haley, held him down, and scrubbed his face clean. Although Craig led the charge, I got my ass kicked by Tippy, because it was my mom's washcloth! He threw the cloth over a telephone wire. There's justice for you!

"Wrong Way Haley" – Ryan; if there was a wrong way to do something, Ryan would do it! And, he had a knack for dragging the rest of us into his little schemes. I remember, on more than one occasion, that Ryan would announce that he was forming a new, exclusive club. And, that if you wanted to be a member, it would cost you twenty-five cents for dues. After he had collected several quarters, miraculously, the club would fold by the following day, and Ryan would spend the money on himself, at the candy store. Scumbag!

"Dead-Eye" – Mickey Callahan; another "Big Kid". He had a droopy eyelid, thus the personal affliction came into play. The "Little Kids" didn't like Mickey very much. He caused a lot of trouble over the years, and reminded me of a weasel. He was always getting his ass kicked by someone.

"Pop-'em Rod" – Rod McNulty: BK. Obvious sophomoric attempt at a penis joke – a staple in our world. Rod was always a good guy. It didn't seem to matter to him how old you were, or "Stature" in the neighborhood. Rod was most notorious for having a false front tooth, which he could take out at any time. He lost his real tooth water skiing, when the tip of the ski hit him right in the mouth.

"Smitty" – Karl Smith. This was given to him by his former boss, at the grocery store we all worked at during our teens. You would regularly hear "Smitty, up front to bag! Smitty, up front to bag!"

"Skunk Cabbage" - the nickname Ted Hanson foisted upon his brother, Ken. He was another gifted athlete, with a rocket for an arm. I remember watching Ken play softball, and the guys on his team getting on his case, because Ken would throw a strike from the deepest part of the outfield, to third base, but might have made the third baseman reach six inches to one side or the other.

Ken was tough. He had to be. He had Teddy as his brother, and Teddy wouldn't stand for second best.

"Gig the Pig" - Greg Caserino. He was an occasional visitor to Delmont Street. I just threw this one in, because I think it's funny. Greg was certifiably insane. He and I always got along, but he always carried himself as if he were the true missing link. We expected to see him walking on his knuckles at any moment. We were careful to not piss him off, because when he snapped, he would light into his victim like the Tasmanian Devil, and never knew when to turn off the attack. Greg used to tell us that he was going to join the World Wrestling Federation when he grew up and, in his word, "BREAK NECKS, BREAK NECKS!!!"

Greg actually wrote a theme song about me, and used to sing it at the top of his lungs, when he'd see me in the school hallways, on the street, wherever:

"Never fear, Eric is always here!

Loyal, truthful, kind, obedient, cheerful, clean, thrifty, clean…

And, o - BEEEEEEE – dient!

And, o – BEEEEEEE – dient!

Errr-IC, ERR-ic!

Aeeeeeeewwwww!"

What can I say? The guy was traveling in his own solar system.

"Chud" – David Laddimore - another visitor. Don't ask me why… He just looked like a chud – a big doofus. He was in the "Special Class" at school, but we let him hang out. Chud and I weren't always friends. As a matter of fact, early on, I was afraid of him. He was much bigger than the rest of us, a couple of years older, and started out by making me his target of abuse, until I decided to stand my ground one day, and found out he wasn't as tough as I thought. I remember the fight ending rather quickly, Chud surrendering, and declaring that there would be a rematch, after he went home to get his "Strong Pills". The rematch never happened. It was after that, that we started hanging out together. The other guys just tolerated him, when he'd come around.

"Our Friend Davids" – My cousin, Kevin, by my mom's sister, my Aunt Adele. When he would show up, somebody would yell: "Hey! It's our friend, Davids!" I guess we thought it sounded like the name of a TV sitcom.

Kevin was always welcomed into our circle of friends. He was another one of those guys that everyone liked. His mom and dad divorced when Kevin and his sister, Heather, were young, so Kevin spent a lot of time around our house. He loved my mom and dad, and they were good to him. He was the closest thing to a brother I would have. I remember dancing around in his basement, listening to his copy of "It's a Gas", which was a free 45 RPM record, which came in an issue of MAD Magazine. We liked it, because grown men were burping, on the record. Very high brow stuff!

"George Walski" – This was the universal name that everyone in the gang used when they ever got into trouble with an adult or a cop, whatever:

> *"What's your name, boy?"*

"George Walski, sir!"

"Where do you live?"

"Delmont Street, sir."

"Well, Mr. Walski, I'm going to call your parents, and tell them what you did!"

(Good luck!)

Chapter Six

Delmont Street Glossary of Terms

The following represents some of the more colorful, well-worn terms uttered by me, and the other "Rhodes Scholars" I called my friends. They may not be G-rated, or politically correct, but it was our vernacular, and it was accepted.

"Bawko" – Clumsy, awkward, moronic,

"Cloppo" – See Bawko

"Shit for Brains" – Can be used to insult or for a term of endearment.

"Assface", "Dumbass", "Douchebag", "Dickface", "Fart Biscuit", "Clankhead"– See Shit for Brains.

"Having a Girl Fit" – If your voice cracks while talking. Typical among pre-teen boys.

"Cheetos Feet" – If you wore orange leather work boots, and got them wet, the color would stain your feet, so your toes looked like Cheetos.

"Pulling a (Last Name Here)" – If someone in the gang did something incredibly stupid, and someone else repeated the same stupid act. For example, if I were to fall down a flight of stairs, and two years from now Karl were to do the same thing, then that would be "Pulling a Mann".

"Shit On" – If someone hit you with a particularly stinging insult, or made you look like a fool, then that was being "Shit On". It was a standard cry among the Gang – "Ahh-hah-hah-hah-HAHHHHH! SHIT ON!"

"Froot of the Loops" – Mrs. Smith confused the famous breakfast cereal with the famous underwear, and the name stuck.

"Ass Breaker" – Think of a "cannon ball" into a swimming pool, only an "A – Breaker" is done with your legs straight out in front of you, so that you're in a sitting position, when you hit the surface of the water. The optimal "breaker" is achieved when your ass and legs hit the water with a slap. If done correctly, it stings like hell.

"Knuckle in the A" – I believe this was developed by Ted Hanson. It required you to swing your arm up behind you, much like a bowling ball delivery, then driving your closed fist into your victim's ass, by leading with the knuckle on your first finger, thus delivering the "Knuckle in the A". Very effective.

"Crockett Cry" – Named after this old guy on my paper route. The guys used to wait until I would ring his doorbell to collect for the paper delivery, and one or more of them would be hiding in the bushes, and scream at the top of their lungs, when Old Man Crockett would answer the door.

This "cry" morphed into a standard in the gang, especially when we would be riding around in a car. We would drive alongside some kid walking home from school or, if we were particularly ballsy, an adult, lean as far out of the window as we could, and scream at the top of our lungs. Then we'd laugh like sadistic idiots, as books, groceries, or the pet dog would go flying, as our victim would lose control of all of their bodily functions.

"Window Shopping" – Our secret code for watching one particular girl in the neighborhood, who shall remain nameless, undress. She always left her curtains open, and always stood right in front of the window. We would line up the lawn chairs, grab the popcorn, and wait for the show to begin. Truth be told, I think she knew we were there.

"Piss Call" – This was designed to catch the victim sleeping. One of us would drop by or call on the victim, thus waking him up, and pissing him off. Larry was the best target for this because odds were in our favor that he'd still be asleep at noon.

Chapter Seven
TV Time

As I had mentioned, we had three channels of black and white television – three and eight on VHF, and thirty on UHF. They represented the "big three" networks – NBC, CBS and ABC. Actually, when the weather conditions were just right, we could get channel 22 out of Springfield, Massachusetts, and channel 18, an independent UHF station.

WTIC Channel Eight was the CBS affiliate out of Hartford, emanating from its studios on Constitution Plaza. Like many local stations of the time, they had their own local kids' shows; the most popular of which was "The Ranger Andy Show". It was popular because it had a live studio audience, and all the kids wanted to be on TV. The set was a mock-up of a ranger station, with a big picture window, that had no glass. The stage director would line up all of the kids, and they would march into the ranger station, while the opening theme song would play, and the credits would roll. The kids were warned not to stick their hands through the window. We all wanted to know why there was no glass. Why was there no glass??? This is real, isn't it?? Please explain!!!

Inevitably, no matter how many times the kids were coached not to, some smartass would lean through the window, waving wildly, totally breaking the aura of the set for the viewers.

Ranger Andy played the banjo, sang songs, played games, and showed Hanna Barbera cartoons. They even gave away parting gifts; usually it was a box of Maypo Oatmeal, or Stateline Potato Chips.

On Fridays, Ranger Andy would have "Joke Day", where he would let the kids in the studio audience tell their favorite joke. One time, a kid told the following, given to him by his older brother:

> *"Why are a frying pan and a woman alike?"*
>
> *"I don't know. Why?"*
>
> *"Because, you have to get both of them hot, before you put the meat in!"*

When the show came back after the emergency commercial break, that kid was mysteriously gone from the audience, never to be heard from, again.

WTIC also had The Milk Show, which was a local American Bandstand-like dance show, hosted by Brad Davis, a local institution who is still on Connecticut radio to this day. And, of course, the sponsor was the Connecticut Dairy Farmers Association. Brad would introduce the latest songs on the charts, while local high school kids would cavort to the rhythm. Then, Brad would extol the virtues of a nice, cold glass of milk. What a wholesome way to spend the afternoon.

WTNH Channel Eight, from New Haven, had The Mister Goober Show, which was my personal favorite. It was like a demented version of Romper Room. I thought he was funny as hell. His sense of humor was more adult, and there was always something that would elicit uproarious laughter from the parents in the studio audience. Whenever he would introduce a cartoon, he would exclaim "Turn the crank, Frank!"

Goober showed the old Clutch Cargo cartoons, which were the one-dimensional cartoons that had the human mouths superimposed on the characters' faces. They were eerie, and politically incorrect by today's standards, but we got a kick out of them.

WVIT, the NBC affiliate, had Colonel Clown, who showed The Three Stooges throughout the show. And who doesn't love a good Stooge short?

On Sunday mornings, Davey and Goliath was on. These were the religious claymation shows, pre-Gumby, which all had a religious moral attached. Goliath was Davey's goofy dog, who always followed after his master, proclaiming "Gee, Daaaaaavey!"

On Tuesday and Wednesday evenings, at 7:30 PM, was time for Batman, with Adam West as the Caped Crusader, and Burt Ward as Robin, the Boy Wonder. The guest villains made the show work – whether it was Burgess Meredith, Frank Gorshin, Caesar Romero, Julie Newmar (Catwoman! Yummy!), or one of the others, Mom and I always watched, and laughed. To this day, I still love that show.

World Wide Wrestling Federation was another staple of ours, watching Chief Jay Strongbow, Pedro Morales, Bruno Sammartino and a host of other behemoths throw each other around the squared circle. We actually got carried away with wrestling. One time, I was wrestling with Karl, and accidently dropped him on his head. I was so shocked to see my friend lying in a heap, I could only respond, by saying *"SHIT!"*

"Mann, you Idiot! You could have killed him!"

"Well, I <u>said</u> Shit!"

I guess I didn't handle panic very well.

<u>Wild, Wild West</u>, <u>Man from U.N.C.L.E.</u>, <u>Get Smart</u>, <u>Captain Kangaroo</u>, <u>Andy Griffith Show</u>, <u>Hawaii Five-O</u>, <u>Mannix</u>, <u>The Beverly Hillbillies</u>, <u>Hogan's Heroes</u>, <u>The Carol Burnett Show</u>, <u>The Dick Van Dyke Show</u>, <u>Gomer Pyle, U.S.M.C.</u>, <u>F Troop</u>, <u>Leave it to Beaver</u>, <u>McHale's Navy</u>, <u>Rowan and Martin's Laugh-In</u>, <u>Green Acres</u>, and <u>Rat Patrol</u> – these were among my favorite shows of the time. And, I don't want to hear any crap about the fact that I didn't watch <u>Star Trek</u>! I put up with a lot of grief from Ted about this, and I'm not going to put up with it, from you! I just didn't like it. I didn't learn to appreciate it until the movies started coming out.

This was also the era of game shows – every channel, every day. Concentration, Jeopardy, Tic Tac Dough, Joker's Wild, Match Game, The Price is Right - just to name a few.

There was no MTV, no E Channel, no celebrity gossip, no reality shows – just entertainment – innocent entertainment. And, every night, at the end of the broadcast day, the National Anthem would play, followed by the famous American Indian test pattern, and the familiar "booooooooooooooooooooooooooooooooop".

Chapter Eight
Ringing Doorbells

In most towns, ringing doorbells was just a way to annoy your neighbors, and get a cheap laugh from watching them run around the outside of their homes, trying to catch "those little brats" in the act.

We, on the other hand, made it an art; something more than the mundane "ding- dong and dash". It was a group activity; an opportunity to work as a team, and enjoy the moment...the majesty.

We would put our own little twists on this great American pastime, such as placing a phonebook between the top of the screen door and the frame, knowing full well that the victim's curiosity would get the best of him, and he would open the door, thus getting bonked on the head with the book.

Matt and I made our own contribution to the "Bell Ringers Hall of Fame", by making the experience more interactive. Remember, this was thirty years before the TV show <u>Jackass</u>, and the like, when we decided to go "face-to-face". We would ring the bell, and when the door was answered, I would start my pitch:

> *"Hello, Madam! My name is George Walski, and I'm collecting magazines for the Manchester Association for Gifted Citizens. And, this is one of the citizens you will be helping. His name is Owen. Say hello, Owen!"*

At this point, Matt, who has been standing obnoxiously close to our unsuspecting homemaker, with a particularly moronic look on his face, says "hello" as only he can:

> *"mmmmmBAAAHHH!"*

At this point, the victim has recoiled, and either retreated to the safety of her house, or run to collect whatever magazines are handy, out of sympathy for poor "Owen". Do you have any idea how hard it is to pull this off without cracking up, while you're listening to the rest of the crew convulsing in the bushes???

Most times, I took on the role of director, casting each role for our montage, rehearsing each actor's role, then setting the staging for our presentation. At any given time, you could answer your front door, and find six or eight boys simultaneously wrestling, singing the National Anthem, making a human pyramid, or hiding one's head inside a turtle-neck sweater, and yelling "I can't find my HEAD!" You know, real thought-provoking stuff!

One night, while attempting another epic bell ringer, Ryan was hiding in the neighbor's trash barrel, waiting to jump out, while David, Karl and some of the other guys were across the street, hiding in the bushes, waiting for the action to take place. I was the designated "ringer". When everyone was set, I rang the bell, jumped off the porch, ran toward the street, tripped over the broken sidewalk, and did a face planter, right in the middle of the street!

While I'm lying there, writhing in pain, the neighbor comes to the door. I proceed to tell the neighbor that I was beat up, trying to stop some kids from vandalizing his house. He wants to give me a ride home, but I heroically decline. This entire time, I'm hearing the sounds of stifled, maniacal laughter emanating from the bushes across the street. Glad I could bring such joy into your lives, you a-holes!

Chapter Nine

Main Street and the State Theater

Main Street was special.

If you were a kid, and you were taking a trip downtown to Main Street, it usually meant something cool was happening. For the kids in my neighborhood, taking the two-mile trek downtown was a weekly ritual, for one of several reasons.

Thursday night was "Family Night". The whole town would turn out. All the stores were open until nine o'clock! Can you believe it??? Marlow's Department Store, Woolworth's, House and Hale's, The Brass Key Restaurant, Regal Men's Shop, Beller's Music Store and several others were open in one big block party. Mom, Dad and all the kids would turn out, park the car, and walk from the top of Center Street down to Charter Oak Street, and back. The beat cop's job was to keep the sidewalks clear, as dozens of people would stop to congregate, and catch up. Your arm would be sore from waving to everyone you knew.

Marlow's was the coolest store around. The décor was circa 1940, and they still had merchandise from that era, and every era since. You could find anything there, and I MEAN anything. If you needed a skate key, Old Man Marlow had it. If you wanted a Super Ball in the original 1960's packaging, he had it! If you needed a sewing needle for a 1950's Singer Sewing machine, Marlow's had it. It was old and dusty and dingy and fun; and we always looked forward to going there.

Although not technically on Main Street, there was another great stop just around the corner on Hartford Road – The Cheney Mills, named after the Cheney Brothers, who founded the silk mills in 1838, and employed a large number of Manchester residents, for years. Truth be told, Manchester probably should have been named "Cheneyville".

Anyway, after the mills had closed in the fifties, one of the buildings was converted to a terrific discount department store, called King's. It had a huge concrete staircase which led to three floors of clothing, toys, housewares, hardware, and fun. It was fresh bags of popcorn and balloons for the kids, and a great place to run and play, while the parents shopped.

Saturday on Main Street was "Everything Day". First thing in the morning, Larry, Karl, David, Ted and I would head down to the Manchester Herald, to turn in our paper route money. Then we'd head up to the Roma Pastry Shop, which opened at nine o'clock sharp, and have hot chocolate and a pastry. Then, it was home to deliver the Saturday paper, lunch, then back downtown for the matinee at the State Theater.

The State Theater was your typical grand, old theater, with a fully-working proscenium stage, used during the old vaudeville era, a free-standing ticket booth, snack bar and balcony. Next door was the Bissell Soda Fountain, which had a huge penny candy counter. The routine went this way – Dad would give my sisters and me a dollar each, and we'd head down to the matinee'. A child's ticket was thirty-five cents, popcorn was fifteen cents, and a soda was a dime. That left forty cents for forty pieces of penny candy.

The candy counter was run on the honor system. We would grab one of those brown paper bags, with the red and green stripes and stock up on Squirrel Nuts, Atomic Fire Balls, Mary Janes, Paper Dots, Bazooka Bubble Gum, Tootsie Rolls, Pixie Sticks, Nikl Nips and licorice whips. We'd then bring the bag to the old man behind the cash register. He'd ask us how many pieces we had taken, and we would tell him, and give him the money; and we never, ever fibbed!

We always kept our fingers crossed that the balcony would be open, as we thought this was incredibly cool, especially if you were sitting in the very front row of the balcony. It was akin to being in the first car of a roller coaster. It was also great for chucking candy at the kids below.

After two features and a half-dozen cartoons, four-hundred maniacs, wired on sugar, were released to the custody of their parents.

The last Saturday of summer vacation meant one thing. It was time for the Pencil Box Matinee' at the State Theater. It was traditionally the busiest day of the year at the theater. The line would start forming early in the morning, work its way around the block, and start around again. This was the one matinee' each year that had two complete showings, so that everyone had a chance to receive their treasure. Every kid would receive a cardboard pencil box, blue for boys, red for girls, complete with two number two pencils, a rubber eraser, a compass, a protractor, and a red and blue pen. It also had a secret drawer in the bottom.

Parents would schedule their vacations around this most-important event. A kid would have to be in a coma not to show up. Kids would show up on crutches, in wheelchairs, and with barf bags, so they wouldn't be left out. You _had_ to be there! If you were to show up on the first day of school, and didn't have your pencil box, you were weird!

We had figured out, early on, that security was not too tight at the State, when I found out that the exit doors at the back of the theater did not completely lock, if they weren't pulled shut from the inside. It was determined, through masterful surveillance on my part, that there was a twenty-second lapse between the end of the coming attractions and the start of the first feature film, when the theater was absolutely dark. We would wait outside the exit, the previews would end, the room would darken, the feature would start, and there would be 10 or 12 new patrons in the front rows, crouching down in the seats, hoping to avoid detection. I don't think any of us ever got snagged.

I even worked there for a short while as an usher, when I was sixteen. We all had to wear black tuxedo jackets, and carry a flashlight, and stock the snack bar, and pick up trash between showings. You know; glamorous stuff! One of the perks was getting to go to the shows for free. What a big shot I was, when I would bring my friends down for a free movie. I used to love to sit in the closed balcony, during my breaks, with a slice of pizza, and take it all in, watching a 30-foot tall Bruce Lee beat up the bad guys, in <u>Enter the Dragon.</u>

Unfortunately, the State had outlasted its usefulness, when the UA Theaters East, the first twin-theater opened at the Manchester Parkade, in the mid-seventies. The State couldn't compete with the 99 – cent ticket price for any show, in this new, sanitary facility, with plenty of parking. It finally closed around 1977, ending the era of the grand, old theater.

The State Theater was where you felt grown up, when your parents let you go by yourself; this is where you brought your first date – saw your first PG rated movie…

This was a real movie theater, on a real Main Street.

Chapter Ten

Winter Sports

At the risk of sounding like my dad, In MY day, we were a heartier lot. No sub-zero temperatures were going to stop US from having fun! Not like today – give the kid a DVD player, and an X-Box, and you don't see him for a week!

Nope! Not us! We were outside – and we would stay there until we started to lose feeling in our extremities – inside, for a quick cup of hot chocolate – outside, until it was time for dinner.

We couldn't wait for the first storm, and in Connecticut, that usually meant the two sweetest words we would ever hear - "School Closings". We would wake up, and immediately turn the radio on, to hear the complete list of Snow Day Closings.

Our fun would manifest itself in several forms. First thing's first - we would have to build a snow fort. This traditionally took place in the Bentley School parking lot, which was down the street from my house. The plows would push all the snow to the corner of the lot, creating a huge mountain for us to work with. Several of us would arrive with shovels, to start constructing a snow fort of epic proportions. No, we never took the easy way out. We had to build a fort that would stand the test of time- a fort that would last forever. Or, until the spring thaw, whichever came first.

We would construct parapets, block walls, a tunnel to a safe room, another which would weave its way for about thirty feet, so we could make a hasty escape – we thought of everything!

Why the escape tunnel? So that we could safely engage in our favorite winter pastime, throwing snowballs at cars! And, we were good at it. See, the snow fort was always in the corner of the school parking lot, which butted up against the intersection of Summit and Hollister Streets, which was a four-way stop. It was like shooting fish in a barrel. The moment an unsuspecting car would pull up to the stop sign, six or ten kids would appear from the confines of the fort, and lay the car to waste with a precision attack which would have made General Patton proud.

Of course, if we happened to catch some working stiff returning home from a hard day at the office, the victim would get pissed off, and chase after us. That's where the tunnel system came in. The car would pull into the parking lot, the driver would exit, climb up to the fort, and find no sign of us. That's because we were hiding in the safe room, giggling our moronic little butts off. If the irate driver happened to find the entrance to our room, we would scoot down the escape tunnel, and pop up about thirty feet away and run like hell!

Another favorite spot for snowballs and cars was the Gallo's house, directly across the street from my house. This was a location that was actually quite sporting, as it required considerable skill. We would stand in the backyard, behind the garage. From that position, we could see the intersection at Summit and Hollister. A car would start through the intersection, and it was our mission to lob our snowballs over the roof of the garage, and perfectly time the arrival of the car and snowball at the same point. The missile would reach the intended target, and the driver never knew from whence it came. It was a thing of beauty, and we were learning about geometry, at the same time!

Of course, it didn't always go smoothly. One time, I'm walking down Delmont Street after dark, and I met up with Jeff Hart, a "Big Kid" in the neighborhood. Now, the strange thing about Jeff was that he had a very domineering mother, who rarely let Jeff hang out with the rest of us. I don't know why – we were wonderful kids - really! I mean, I can't remember three times during my entire childhood that Jeff came out to play with the rest of us – not baseball, football, nothing!

And, here he was, standing right in front of me! I told him that I was surprised to see him out at night. He told me that his mom and dad had gone out for the evening, and he decided to sneak out. The kid was three years older than I was! He wanted to have some fun, before the "Warden" returned. I thought for a moment, and then asked him the monumental question:

"Wanna throw snowballs at cars?"

And, then this poor, deprived child gave me an answer I'll never forget – an answer that <u>still</u> sends chills down my spine:

"I've never done that before."

I valiantly steadied myself on wobbly legs, visibly stunned by this horrific revelation! When I regained my composure, I had a new resolve! I <u>knew</u> this chance meeting was fate – destiny, if you will – ordained by a higher, GREATER POWER THAN MYSELF!!!

I MUST SAVE THIS BOY FROM HIS POOR, MEANINGLESS LIFE!!!

I took Jeff behind the Gallo's garage, and proceeded to show him the finer points of this lost art. An anonymous driver stopped at Summit and Hollister, and slowly approached "ground zero". With perfect timing, I deftly lofted my frozen grenade over the garage, and "boomp", found the hood of the passing car. We ducked down, and giggled like a couple of idiots while the car slowed, paused, and then continued on its way. Success!

Now, it was Jeff's turn; and he was eager to become Manchester's newest juvenile delinquent. Headlights appeared out of the darkness, and came to a stop at the corner. The moment of truth was drawing near – the tension mounted. The car was moving - getting closer. Jeff's anticipation grew. It was TIME! It was TIME! THROW IT!!!

POW! Right in the windshield! The car screeched to an abrupt halt. Something was different...

That's when the bright, red light on top of the car started to shine...

I never realized how fast or how far I could run though knee-deep snow, when terror was my prime motivator. The unlucky bastard hit a cop car!!! Through a dozen backyards, and Jeff was right on my heels, repeating *"My mom is gonna kill me, my mom is gonna kill me!"*

Oh, Mister Policeman circled the block several times; he even attempted a short foot chase, but thought better of it. About fifteen minutes later, he gave up trying to hunt down such dangerous fugitives.

Jeff was done. The fun was over. He turned, and started the walk back to his house, never saying a word...

...I don't recall ever seeing Jeff Hart outside after that – ever.

Freddy Corrado was a true athlete, with a thunderbolt for a pitching arm. Nobody wanted to stand in the batter's box against him. But, we REALLY feared him in winter. That's when he would make a batch of his custom snowballs, that the kids in the neighborhood would call "Corrado Specials". They were unconventionally small – about the size of a golf ball – and, if Freddy ever hit you in the leg with one of those, you'd be walking with a limp for a week. Freddy's dad, whom I affectionately call "Doctor Bob", used to tell Freddy that, if he insisted on throwing snowballs, "…at least aim low, so that you don't put someone's eye out!"

We all loved sledding. The more speed and danger, the better we liked it. There were two favored locations for sledding. The first was the "Bobsled Track" in the woods beyond the end of Delmont Street. This was a track that we built that careened between the trees, and actually had two banked curves that, if taken at the right speed, you actually found yourself sideways. We all used the plastic Coleco-brand sleds. You know; the flat, rudderless sled with the bright yellow handles. These were best, because the rudders on the old Flexible Flyer sleds chewed up the hill you were using it on, and we had worked too hard to perfect this track!

We didn't merely slide down the hill – No! That was too boring! We would start four or five sleds from different tributaries, leading to a common meeting place on the hill, where we would proceed to smash the crap out of each other all the way to the bottom. The bigger the battle, the better…

One time, a bunch of us were in the midst of one of our epic "Battle Royals", when Tom Gallasso, another kid who was on the fringes of our group, decided to dive bomb from his sled, on top of me. Of course, I couldn't allow that! I simply grabbed him by the front of his jacket, and held him straight out to one side, as we slid by an oak tree – BLAM!

When we all reached the bottom of the hill, all we saw were Gallasso's arms and feet protruding from both sides of the tree, and some muffled sobbing. He was okay, though. Heck, after all these years, he barely *has* a problem with the uncontrolled drooling.

The *big* hill for sledding was located at Center Springs Park. This hill seemed like it was a quarter-mile long or more, about 100 yards wide, and lighted for night sledding. At the bottom of the hill was a brook that more than one kid would have to be rescued from on a weekly basis, as they overshot their landing point. This was a hugely - popular family hangout, and probably still is. I can remember dad dragging the family toboggan up that hill time and time again, loading it up with the neighborhood kids, and sending us careening down this mammoth peak to crash into unsuspecting winter revelers gathered below.

One time, when I was about nine, I talked my mom into taking a ride down this hill, on the back of my Flexible Flyer, while I steered. We were flying, when we hit a bump, near the bottom of the hill. Mom fell off, and landed flat on her butt, tearing the back out of her pants, her girdle, everything. As she sat there, bare-assed in the snow, one of the fathers came to her aid and lent her a coat to wrap around her, until she reached home.

One night, Karl Smith and I carried twin blue plastic Coleco-brand boats up to the top of the hill. We sat in one, and locked the other on top of us, making something like a clam shell. We pointed our new, high-tech rocket cylinder toward the ski jump, which was halfway down the hill, and took off.

I don't know how fast we were traveling when we hit the jump – I just remember the audible "gasp" from the gathered crowd, as we went airborne. I remember thinking how peaceful I felt as the wind whistled by, as our capsule started to rotate, and we were now upside-down. I can't be certain, but I think I heard Karl muttering a "Hail Mary" under his breath. We hit the ground with tremendous force, and the capsule exploded…

When I came to, I was face down in the snow. I lifted my head, and looked around with my one unfrozen eye, my eyeglasses hanging from one ear, and saw one of the boats, and Karl's leg dangling out of it. I called to my fallen friend, "Karl… Karl, are you okay?" Slowly, a gloved hand rose from the boat, producing a "thumbs up" sign, and slowly sank back out of sight.

The crowd cheered with delight and reverence, as we gathered our composure, and slowly hobbled off into the night, forever emblazoning this moment on the folklore of Center Springs Hill, never to be duplicated by mere mortals, again.

Chapter Eleven
"Hello! My Name's Eric, and I'm a Moron!"

My parents trusted me. And, for the most part, I didn't give them any reason not to – at least none they ever knew.

During the winter months, doing my paper route was an ordeal. There were times when it was ass-biting cold, and walking for an hour and a half in the dead of winter exacerbated that point.

More afternoons than not, when I arrived home, I would start a fire in the fireplace by gathering logs off of our wood pile, behind the house. Mom and Dad knew this, they trusted me, and I was good at it…

…until this one time.

I came home from delivering my papers, on a particularly damp winter afternoon. As usual, I went to get some wood for the fire, but found that the wood pile was also wet. I searched for some dry pieces, and took them into the house. Claudia was in the kitchen, boiling a pot of water to cook spaghetti, for the family dinner.

After several attempts at starting the fire, using kindling, newspaper, and several matches, it just wouldn't light. That's when a "brilliant" idea popped into my head – go into the garage, and get some gasoline! That'll start the fire! I figured I would get a little bit, drip it on the logs, and everything would be fine.

I retrieved about an ounce of gas, poured into a plastic cup, and carried it into the house. I walked over to the fire place, kneeled over the hearth, and attempted to dribble the gasoline onto the logs. That's when the first few drops hit the hidden glowing ember.

I had no reason to believe that this was the stupidest idea I had ever had, and was dumbfounded when the flame jumped right up to the cup that was still in my hand, engulfing it, my hand, and part of my coat sleeve. I threw the cup into the fireplace, and the flames exploded with a "WHOOSH".

The hearth was on fire, the fireplace broom was on fire, and the LIVING ROOM CARPET WAS ON FIRE! I screamed for Claudia to help, as I tried to beat out the flames with my coat. Claudia ran into the room, screamed, ran back into the kitchen, grabbed the pot of boiling spaghetti on the stove, ran back into the living room, and with one well-placed shot, put out the entire inferno.

We stood back, still in hysterics, to survey the damage. Other than water, spaghetti, and a little smoke damage, the only thing that was ruined was the living room rug. I had melted a section about a foot long, and about four inches wide. I was convinced that Mom and Dad would kill me.

The two of us scrambled to clean up the mess, and did a great job, if I do say so myself. By the time our parents got home, everything was back to normal, except for the throw rug that was strategically placed over the burned spot on the rug.

When Mom and Dad arrived home, I immediately told them what happened, and showed them the burn mark. Amazingly, they were pretty cool about it. No yelling, no punishment, no nothing. I just got a lecture from Dad about pulling such a bonehead stunt, and how I should be grateful for having a sister like Claudia. He was right. It <u>was</u> a bonehead stunt, and I was glad that I had a sister like Claudia, and that <u>she</u> had the poise under pressure to save the family house, and bail out her moron of a brother.

Chapter Twelve
The Great Bentley School Baseball Caper

Every spring, I wait with baited breath for the familiar to be new again – the aroma of newly-mown grass, a well-oiled mitt, and the burning smell that emanates from a wooden baseball bat, when a fastball is fouled off. It's time for the Great American Sport.

We lived for baseball. It was not out of the ordinary to find a great number of us at Bentley School, first thing in the morning, playing game after game all day, until it was too dark to see the ball cross the plate, or the "moms" would start hollering for us to come home for dinner, where we'd share our day with our parents:

"What'd you do today, Son?"

"I played baseball all day!"

"How'd you do?"

"I hit fifty-seven home runs!"

"That's my boy!"

This was not really a baseball field, in the typical sense. The infield was a combination of hard-packed dirt, dust, rocks and broken blacktop. The outfield was all blacktop. The outfield wall was actually the back of the school, with the school auditorium's outer wall doing double-duty as the center field wall. This is where I insisted upon positioning myself during games, as I envisioned myself as Carl Yastrzemski, playing in front of the "Green Monster" at Fenway Park, leaping to make a backhanded catch against the wall, or perfectly fielding a hit on a carom, and throwing out the runner at second base. It rarely happened, but I liked to believe it did.

As fields go, it wasn't much to look at; but, it was ours...

But, there was something missing. There were no numbers on the outfield wall, marking the distance from home plate! How could we possibly be expected to play like the pros, if we didn't play on a field like the pros???

So, one rainy Sunday, I walked up to the school with a standard, 3-foot yardstick, and proceeded to measure the distance from home plate to the left, center and right field walls. Do you know how hard, and how stupid, it is to take these measurements with a yardstick?

The following Saturday, at around two in the morning, I snuck out of the house, with a can of white paint, and made a beeline for Bentley School. With tremendous sincerity, and very little dexterity, I proceeded to make our ball field complete, by tattooing the back of the school with the numbers that meant so much to us – 225 feet to left, 160 feet to center, and 240 down the right field line. When I was finished, I stood back and proudly surveyed the fruits of my labor. In <u>my</u> mind, this was history. This was timeless. Years from now, I thought, generation after generation of baseball enthusiasts would play on this field, and know how far they had hit the ball, and have the same thrills that we all had, imagining we were our favorite big league players. I had performed a great humanitarian task; I had changed lives for the better; I HAD DONE A GREAT THING…!

WRONG!!!

Several hours later, the guys showed up to play ball, and saw the new addition to the playground we called home, and tongues started wagging. The word got around the neighborhood in one afternoon. Then, came Monday morning...

I never saw it coming – I was the last to know. Mrs. Woods, the Principal of Bentley School, arrived for work, saw that her school had been "defaced", and the investigation started. Teachers were instructed to question their respective classes to see if they could develop any leads. One of the neighborhood kids, not part of our gang, took a shot at notoriety, and yelled out "Eric Mann did it!"

After that, it was just a matter of time. Almost everyone in our gang was questioned, and they all buckled. Then, it was my turn. I was called into the office, to find Mrs. Woods, and an investigator from the School Superintendent's office. And, they poured it on, pretty thick. I asked them what made them think I was the culprit. They had every detail. The guys – MY friends – had folded like a collection of cheap pup tents. COWARDS!

I was sunk. I didn't try to deny it. What I didn't understand was why they were making such a big deal out of this! After all, didn't I just improve the building? I wasn't being destructive; I was performing a service! Hell, what about all the "bad" graffiti which already covered these walls? There were several fairly nasty curse words strewn about, and they didn't investigate those! Things like "Matt eats this" or "David sucks that!" And, I'm sure that several of the other spray painted suggestions were illegal in several states! Why me???

"Because, you got CAUGHT!"

They called my parents. Mom was pissed. Dad was actually pretty cool about it, when he came to pick me up at the school, but I remember him giving me a look that said "Bonehead, what the Hell were you thinking???" My punishment? I would have to spend the weekend scrubbing the numbers off the walls. My Dad tried to explain that the odds of cleaning the numbers off the school were slim, since I used oil-based paint on porous red brick. Mrs. Woods didn't care. She wanted to teach me a lesson. So, there I was, for two days, with my dad right beside me, scrubbing the bricks with a wire brush and paint remover. The numbers never did come off. I just smudged them, a little.

Ted Hanson called me one day, to tell me that he brought his son, Joe, by the school, and told him about the legend of the Great Bentley School Baseball Caper, and the "mental midget" who pulled it off. It's been more than thirty years; Mrs. Woods has been gone for some time, may she rest in peace.

The school was recently demolished. Ted called me that day. He cried. I guess I did, too. It was a memory of simpler times, no grown-up worries; and, we were young.

And, all that mattered was baseball.

Chapter Thirteen

The Woods

Earlier, I had mentioned that Delmont Street was a "dead end". At the end of the street was a cow pasture – a remnant of one of the original farms in the center of town. Beyond the pasture lurked "The Woods" – several acres of trees, hills, and a running brook, which would serve as one of our playgrounds for most of our youth. What a great backdrop for playing "guns", or catching tadpoles, or building forts. It was our sanctuary. I truly do not remember one time that one of our parents ever ventured into this hallowed ground. Either they respected our privacy, or they believed that we had shallow graves dug for all of them.

When I was around ten years old, several acres of the far corner of the woods were sold to a local developer, Charles Porticello, who decided to build an apartment complex. We were pissed! How dare he cut into our fun times???? We had to take action! This was WAR!

Over the next several days, we did everything we could to disrupt progress – dirt bombs, rocks, water balloons, dirty names – it didn't matter! We kept pelting the construction crew. Of course, they chased us and called the cops, and we were eventually caught. We told them why we were so mad, and they went easy on us, as long as we promised to knock it off.

In the end, the new apartment buildings didn't eat up all of our woods, and we thought that this was a moral victory. Maybe our epic battles did make a difference… We were ten! What did we know about zoning?

Anyway, as I said, we used to build forts in the woods. And, I'm not talking about some rinky dink "lean to" with some branches piled on it. Nooooo! These forts were always a major construction job. And, if some sheets of plywood or cinder blocks from a nearby construction site happened to make their way into the project, so be it.

The grandest of these forts was a design built by David Corrado, which was actually two stories tall, with four rooms, and an escape tunnel. I mean, by fort standards, this thing was so big, I thought he was going to need a permit! And, it was cool! It was our place to hang out.

We'd rush home, grab a bag lunch, and scurry back, then spend the day doing all of our important planning – when was the next shipment of firecrackers coming in? Who's going to the movies this week? Has anybody stolen a copy of their dad's Playboy magazine?

You know, important stuff!

And, we would try to keep it as confidential as possible, for if the wrong person found out about it, it would be all over. I think this fort actually lasted about four months, until Mr. Earl, owner of the property, decided to visit one day, and saw this monstrosity looming in front of him. He had it torn down, almost immediately. No rhyme, no reason – it was on his land.

Grownups! What did they know?

One day, Matt Haley and I were playing in the woods, pretending to be soldiers by using a couple of sticks as rifles. We were up on a hill which butted up against the backyard of this elderly couple, when we heard them yelling at us to get off of their property. Well, I guess we chose to taunt them a little, by ducking in and out of the trees, waving at them, and generally act like a couple of little assholes. After a couple of minutes, we were tired of this game, and walked back down the hill, and ran into Ryan Haley, who excitedly said *"Hey! Look what I got! FIRECRACKERS!"*

Yep! He had four unopened packs of Black Cats; found in the underwear drawers of many a connoisseur of mayhem and destruction. Let the fun commence! For about the next fifteen minutes we were having a great time blowing stuff up with this illegal "contraband", as we walked through the woods without a care in the world…

…until I saw the badge. There, on the trail in front of us, peeking out from behind a tree, was a Manchester cop, waiting for us to get close enough, so he could grab us. That's when instinct took over. I grabbed Ryan and Matt by their shirts, spun them around, and yelled *"RUN!"* Nobody hesitated - We took off. Ryan asked why we were running. I yelled *"COP!"*

VOOM! The afterburners were lit, and we ran for our lives. It was every man for himself. Ryan dove into some bushes, and starting burying his firecrackers. Matt followed me through some backyards, and out to Hollister Street, right into the middle of a semi-circle of police cars, several officers, guns drawn. I got the order to "freeze". Matt tried to blend in with a group of kids playing in the garage, but the cops didn't buy it, and called him out. Matt lost it, and started sobbing *"I didn't do nothing!"*

We were interrogated by the cops right there on the street. They repeatedly asked us where we hid the guns, and I kept explaining that there were no guns; that we were shooting off firecrackers.

> *"Well, the old couple up the hill said they saw you point rifles at them!"*

Payback's a bitch. We acted like a couple of smart asses, and got caught in our own stupidity. The police were pretty cool about it. We showed them where Ryan hid the firecrackers, and they didn't even tell our parents. What a break!

When it was all over, Ryan finally came out of hiding, all pissed off because we told the cops where his stash was. He never did have his priorities together. And, what did we learn from this little episode? Nothing! Except maybe not to point sticks at old people.

Give up fireworks??? You must be crazy!

Chapter Fourteen
Speaking of Fireworks…

Boys and fireworks never turn out well. Somewhere during the fun, someone is going to pull a bonehead stunt, and end up blowing something up, or something off.

I almost lost two fingers and a thumb, when I had Karl light a firecracker with a short fuse, while I attempted to throw it. It blew up, just as I released it, leaving me temporarily deaf in my right ear, and raising three huge blood blisters on my digits. Close call. I was lucky – stupid and lucky.

One time, a new shipment of crackers came into the neighborhood. Everybody ended up with a supply. With Karl in tow, we brought our new acquisition to my house, to "divvy them up". When we walked in the house, we showed my dad what we had. He laid down the law, immediately:

> *"Eric, I'm only going to warn you this once. Do NOT blow those off around this house! Do you understand me?"*

Or course, I was in total agreement. I knew he wasn't kidding. Karl and I went up to my bedroom, to watch television. It was a warm summer evening, and I had my window open. Dad was in his room, which shared a common wall with mine, watching television, also.

Unbeknownst to Karl and me, Larry and Teddy, who also took possession of their share of two-inch boomers, followed us to my house, and were now lurking outside, below my window. Of course, this wasn't an opportunity they would <u>ever</u> allow to slip by, and took full advantage of the situation, by tossing a lit firecracker up to my window. "Ka-BLOOEY!"

Karl and I just about shit ourselves, we were so startled. But, the <u>real</u> fun was just about to start! That's when I heard my dad, bellowing from the other room:

> *"God-damned little son-of-a-bitch!"*

The next thing I know, my bedroom door explodes off of the hinges, courtesy of Dad's size 9 ½, and he's taking his belt off, ready to drastically shorten my meaningless little life:

> "What did I tell you about firecrackers in the house???"
>
> "I didn't, Dad! I swear it wasn't me!"
>
> "Bullshit! You think I'm deaf??? I _know_ what I heard!"

Dad made a lunge at me, and Karl proceeded to do one of the bravest things I had ever seen – He jumped in front of Dad. Put his hands up in front of him, and quickly told him what happened:

> "Eric didn't do it, Mr. Mann! Someone outside just tossed a firecracker up here! Look! We haven't even opened ours, yet!"

With that, Dad paused. Almost instantly, the red left his eyes, and he dropped his hands, letting the lethal piece of leather drop to his side. He just pointed a threatening finger at me, without uttering another word, as if to say *"You were lucky, this time!'* He turned around and walked back to his room. I leaned out the window, without actually seeing the culprits, and muttered *"You Assholes!",* knowing full well who I was talking about.

The air was silent, except for the insane, muttered laughter of two douchebags in the bushes.

Chapter Fifteen
The Great Foot Race

Every kid in the neighborhood wanted this new squirt gun. It was definitely cool. It was green plastic, in the shape of brass knuckles. The water supply fit in the palm of your hand, and it shot a stream of water thirty to forty feet long. It was great for drive-by soakings while riding your bike. This wonder of modern science soon became a staple in every boy's arsenal. If you didn't own one, you were at a severe tactical disadvantage.

I rode my bike to the Memorial Corner Store, which was where we went to blow some of our paper route money, and bought this "weapon of mass destruction". I couldn't even wait until I got home to fill it with water; I rode across the street to the gas station, and used their water hose to arm myself with a full supply of liquid ammo. And, I went out, looking for my first victim.

Not a one! None of the guys were around! The chance to show off my new acquisition was quickly slipping away! What a jip! What good was having this beautifully constructed work of art, if I couldn't torment some innocent schmo! Dejectedly, I decided to go home.

And there, as if my prayers were being answered, I found the ultimate patsy – a trophy that would ensure my place in the annals of "Kiddom" forever – my dad – lying in his favorite chaise lounge, reading the newspaper under the maple tree, in our own backyard. This was just too good to pass up!

With the stealth of a ninja fighter, I hopped the fence on the side of the house, and crept up behind the chimney. This gave me a clear shot at my intended target, lying there, with his back to me, like an unsuspecting wildebeest, who was about to be devoured by the almighty lion. After saying a short prayer to the gods of mischief, I raised my weapon, and fired. It was beautiful! A perfect arching stream flew majestically across the yard, and landed dead-center, into the folds of my father's newspaper.

He didn't react. He just turned the page, and kept on reading. Was he ignoring me?? I shot again; and again, soaked dad's paper. This time, with little or no emotion is his voice, without leaving his comfy perch, he responded:

> "Eric, I know that's you. I'll advise you to stop now, or suffer the consequences."

Here was my dad – the man who had done so much for me, and the rest of the family. The man who supported us; who got up at the crack of dawn, every single day, breaking his back to give us a better life than he had. It made me stop and think. Didn't he deserve a peaceful Saturday? Was I overstepping the bounds of human decency? Was I encroaching upon my loving father's personal space???

NAHHH!

"Squirt"!!

That did it! I had crossed the line! Dad slowly rose from his chair, folded his paper, slammed it to the ground, and bolted at me! I took one look at the vengeance in his eyes, and took off running. I leapt the fence, thinking I would be safe, but no – he came right over the top, and kept on coming! I took off down Summit Street – he was right behind me! I turned left on Delmont Street – he was <u>still there!</u> How long could he keep up this pace? We ran by the Haley's house. Mr. Haley was on the front lawn, saw what was going on, and yelled:

"Get him, Irv! Kill him!"

We turned the corner, and ran down Clifton Street. By this time, kids were following us on bikes, cheering us on! How much more could he take???

A quick left on Hollister Street, and we were in the home stretch. He <u>had</u> to be ready to drop! The crowd was swelling. A final left turn, back onto Summit Street! This stubborn old man had chased me around the entire block! <u>Surely</u>, he would give up, once we had reached the Mann Family homestead!

No such luck. We passed the house, and were starting the second lap, when I ran out of gas, and collapsed on the neighbor's lawn. "I give! I give!" I pleaded.

"Not good enough!" Dad proclaimed, sat on my chest, and proceeded to dump the contents of my squirt gun on my face. Just about this time, Mr. Speck, our neighbor, opened his front door.

"Hey Irv! How's it going?"

"Good Don. Hey! Can I borrow your hose?"

"Sure. Here ya go! Just turn it off, when you're done."

Mr. Speck walked back in the house, and closed the door, as if this were an everyday occurrence! Dad then proceeded to pay me back for this, and every other practical joke I ever played on him. He almost drowned me that day, taking great enjoyment in blasting me in the face, down my pants, everything.

When he finally called it quits, I knew who the better "Mann" was. As I lay there, covered with mud, out of breath, and struggling to regain my dignity in front of two dozen laughing kids, I watched Dad walk back to the house, through a gauntlet of appreciative, admiring parents, who were living vicariously through my father's actions.

I threw the squirt gun away.

Chapter Sixteen

"My Dad Can Lick Your Dad!"

This outrageous statement was heard more than once over the years in our neighborhood. Chalk it up to a son's pride. The truth was that the majority of us had no facts to back up this statement. Most of us had never seen their dad in a fight… except me.

I was about ten, and one of my bedroom windows was on the south side of the house. Through that window, I could see the street light in the front of our house, on Summit Street. Across the street was the Gallo's house, and this was Connie Gallo's high school graduation night. And, Connie decided to have a few friends over for a little party. Only problem was, about 150 kids crashed the party, and there were cars, and partiers, and an abundance of noise.

Mom and Dad were pretty tolerant of what was going on across the street; after all, it <u>was</u> a special occasion. But, there's only so much that my dad was going to tolerate. After all, it was a school night, and he had three small kids. He also had to get up for work the next day.

So, here it is, approaching eleven o' clock at night, and there's a group of drunken idiots hanging out under the street light, in front of our house. Pretty soon, I heard Dad get out of bed, march downstairs, and open the front door. I leaned out my bedroom window, just in time to see Dad approach this overly-obnoxious group of revelers, and try to reason with them:

> *"Hey guys! I know you're just trying to have a good time, but it is rather late, and we've got three kids who have to get up for school. So, would you mind taking it somewhere else?"*

That's when one of the braver, more-stupid members of the group, who was around 19 or 20 years old, chose to become argumentative:

> *"Yeah? And, what happens if we don't leave?"*

Dad kept his cool:

> *"I'm asking you nicely; I'm treating you with respect. Don't turn this into something we're both going to regret. Now, take it somewhere else!"*

Dead silence. With that, Dad turned around, and walked back into the house, shut the door, and went back to bed. A few minutes later, the noise level had returned to its previous level. Now, Dad's REALLY pissed off! Again, he jumped out of bed, marched downstairs, and opened the front door. This time, however, he was greeted by a little surprise – there was "Mister Bigmouth Brave Guy" taking a leak on the bushes in front of our house, while his friends are laughing. When he saw my dad, he smirked at him, zipped up, and walked back to the assumed safety of his friends.

Now, my dad was a pretty easy-going guy, and it took an awful lot to get him mad, but now he had a head full of steam, when he stomped up to the gang, and got nose-to-nose with the "little shit" who just violated the sanctity of our home:

> *"Have you lost your little mind, or are you just stupid? I asked you nicely to leave, and you piss on my house?? This is your last chance! Leave now, or I'll <u>make</u> you leave!"*

What happened next was something of folklore – something you only see in the movies. This mental midget chose this moment to make one of the biggest mistakes of his relatively short life – he took a swing at my dad!

In one quick, effortless move, Dad ducked out of the way, and hit "Mister Bigmouth Brave Guy" in the jaw with a right cross. The punk hit the ground like a ton of bricks. One punch and he was out! His friends let out an audible gasp. Dad stepped back and stared at the others, ready for an onslaught that never came. It was all over.

In a tone that still sends chills down my spine, Dad commanded the others:

"Now, get this shit off of my lawn!"

Their collective egos bruised, this pack of post-teen wussies picked up their still-unconscious friend, got in their cars, and took off, never to be seen again.

I was both shocked and proud. Dad turned, looked up, and saw me watching from my window, and said to me, in his most-fatherly tone:

"Eric, go to bed!"

Do you <u>think</u> I was going to argue with him???

Chapter Seventeen
Just Not My Day

So, I'm 14-years-old, and I'm playing Junior Alumni Baseball, in Manchester, Connecticut. As much as I wanted to be, I wasn't a great player. I was okay, but my eyes were never good enough, at the plate.

That being said, my team is playing against a team where the star pitcher was Jim Carney, a tall, athletic kid, who could really pitch. Now, I've known Jim for years, as we took drum lessons from the same teacher, and became friends over six years of Saturday morning lessons. But, that didn't count on the field.

I step into the batter's box for my first at-bat of the day, look out to the mound, and Jim gives me a sly, little grin. His first pitch nailed me right in the shoulder, and I take first, staring Jim down, while walking up the baseline.

A couple of innings later, back in the box, I get drilled in the forearm. Now, my dad, the coach, and the people in the stands are voicing their disapproval. The umpire actually warned Jim that one more hit batter would mean an ejection from the game.

My third and final at-bat had arrived. There was Jim, still on the mound. I was truly hesitant to step in. Would he be insane enough to do it again, or was everyone overreacting to a bad coincidence? Whatever the case may be, I had to be brave.

As if being overly careful, Jim came nowhere near me, and the count went to 3 and 1. The next pitch was almost dead center down-the-pipe, and I smashed a one-hopper to short. The ball ricocheted off the dirt, and smacked the shortstop square in the chest. I sprinted up the first base line, while watching the man at short scramble to recover the ball. I safely reached the bag, went beyond it by a couple of feet, and turned inward, toward second base. I looked down toward the shortstop, just in time to see him uncork an off-balance throw, which hit me right in the crotch!!!

The wind rushed out of my lungs, and I hit the dirt like a ton of bricks. Then, that familiar pain, that every male knows too well, rushed over my entire body. For the next several minutes, I was an island unto myself, rolling around in the dirt, moaning and holding onto what was left of my most-sensitive area, not concerned how I looked to the masses in attendance.

A hush had fallen over the crowd, as my coach and my dad ran over to see if they could help. The crowd was waiting with baited breath to see if I would recover. My dad kneeled next to me, and with the proper amount of parental concern, asked his fallen pride-and-joy:

"Where did it hit you, son?"

I mustered up all the energy I could, and with incredulity in my voice and tears in my eyes, I blurted out the first thing to come to mind:

"RIGHT IN THE NUTS!"

The crowd lost their collective minds. Fathers and kids were hysterical. Moms were shocked by such language. I looked up at coach and Dad, and they are suppressing their own laughter! I told them to get me out of there. They helped me to my feet, and I limped off the field, still smarting from this direct hit, to a chorus of applause and laughter.

Like I said, this was just not my day!

Chapter Eighteen
Things Your Kids Could Never Do Today

It's no secret that times have changed; that the things we did as kids would never be allowed today. We never wore helmets when we rode our bikes, and nobody died. We used to fling lawn darts around the backyard, and nobody caught one in the eye. We used to camp out in the woods, with no parental supervision, and always came home in one piece. We went Trick-or-Treating from door to door without fear of abduction. Our existence, for the most part, was carefree – no planned play dates, no cell phones, no hovering parents.

When we were kids, we thought nothing of climbing aboard the bus, in Manchester, and traveling to downtown Hartford, for a day of mischief in the capital city. For a quarter, we could go on this big adventure, without our parents cramping our style. And, it was <u>so</u> far away! Ten miles!

We would jump out at Constitution Plaza, and go to Sage Allen's Department Store, and eat in the cafeteria. We would go G. Fox's Department Store, and ride the elevators, and chase each other through the store. If it was the Christmas season, we would look at the light display on the plaza, and buy presents. You know, nothing spectacular; but, we thought we were grown up.

Then, it was back on the bus to Manchester, to make it home in time for dinner. That's when Mom or Dad would ask:

> "So, what did you do today?"
>
> "Oh, nothing much. We just went to Hartford."
>
> "Oh, that's nice."

If that were to happen today, the parents would have the kid in therapy, trying to determine his motivation.

Unlike today, our parents didn't play "taxi Service" for us. If we wanted to go anywhere, regardless of the mileage, we rode our bikes. They were our lifeline, our freedom. You could be anything and go anywhere, if you had a good bike.

I had three different bikes throughout my youth – one was a 28 – inch Schwinn, which was my favorite do anything, knockaround bike, until it was stolen. The next one was a Ross banana bike – candy apple purple, with a gold and silver sparkle seat, with a 3-speed shifter on the cross bar. It was beautiful. I wish I still had it. Later on, I would graduate to a Triumph ten-speed racer, but that was in my teen years.

Anyway, miles didn't matter. We would peddle three or four miles, in the heat of summer, to go to Globe Hollow, which was a pond-like public pool, in the south end of town. We would spend all day, swimming out to the raft, running around, checking out the girls, buying frozen Zero Bars from the snack bar, drowning a close friend… It was great.

Daredevil stunts on bikes were always acceptable. And, as previously stated, we never wore helmets! Not like today, where mommy's little darling has padding from head to toe, just to ride on the driveway. We used to try some crazy shit. And, most of the time, if it was <u>really</u> insane, you could bet that Ryan "Wrong Way" Haley would be involved.

One time, Ryan brought his sister's tricycle to the top of "Hollister Big Hill", the biggest hill around, on the far-east end of Hollister Street. Like the moron that I am, I let Ryan talk me into standing on the back of the trike, while he drove like a maniac, wildly weaving back and forth, down the hill. I was so scared that I jumped off, and received a major case of road rash. I didn't heal for weeks.

Another time, we took our bikes to the woods off of Wadsworth Street, where there was a dirt path that wove blindly down a hill, eventually arriving at a dirt mound which, when jumped at the right speed, would send you airborne for a distance of about twenty feet, ten feet off of the ground. Ryan came screaming down the hill, peddling like a deranged gerbil on a wheel, hit the jump, went wide, and crashed into the top of a small tree, about ten feet down the hill. When we caught up to him, Ryan was hanging from the tree, upside down, by one leg. His bike was lying in a heap, about eight feet below. We eventually got him out of the tree.

If it was too hot, too far, too cold, or too wet to ride bikes, we never hesitated to hitchhike. I would hitch all over town, and people would actually stop. Once, a Manchester Police Officer actually gave me a ride across town! Another time, the high school vice principal! Amazing! It was acceptable. It was safe. It was another era.

I can't remember the last time I've actually seen someone hitching. At least, someone who didn't look like he was just released from prison...

My friends and I used to "camp out" in my backyard, and then wander around the neighborhood at all hours of the night. We didn't get into trouble; we just thought it was cool to wander around. Besides, how else could we collect materials to build our forts?

Halloween was great! And, I mean great! And, for the most part, our costumes were homemade. The "fall back" costume, when you were stuck for an idea, was to get your dad's old flannel shirt, a pair of baggy pants, and an old hat, and go as a bum. We would smear black shoe polish on our faces to make a beard. Other costumes were usually the store-bought kind, with the plastic face mask, with the eye holes cut out, held in place with that flimsy rubber band. On any given night, there would be a couple dozen Supermans, with the black spit curl on the forehead – as many Batmans, Barbies, G.I Joes, and Incredible Hulks. Two problems with these masks – you couldn't see, and you sweated like hell. After an hour, the masks usually came off, which destroyed the illusion, causing confusion among the neighbors, doling out the candy:

> "And, what are <u>you</u> supposed to be, little boy?"

Coolest costume I ever saw, was a guy dressed all in white, with black block letters jumbled up, all over his outfit. When I asked him what he was going as, he told me "Dyslexia".

We would walk for miles, trick-or-treating in every neighborhood we could imagine. We would all carry pillow cases, to hold our booty, fill them to the point that we couldn't carry them any longer, go home, dump them out, and head out, again. No crappy little plastic pumpkins for us! Back then, the families would pass out full-sized candy bars, apples, wax lips, Nik'l Nips and money. No parents had to escort us – it was our night of freedom. When the evening was over, we'd head back to our homes, and sort our treasures by size and type. The chocolate bars always went in the freezer, to make them last longer. You just hoped that your dad didn't have a sweet tooth.

We used to play tackle football, again with no pads or helmets. It was especially fun to play in the snow. Sure, there were some injuries, but nothing too severe. I guess the worst was when we were playing a team from Elro Street, on the Manchester High School field. During one game, Jay Charles, from Elro Street, suffered a broken collar bone. The bigger problem was the fact that the field is behind a ten-foot high, locked fence. So, when Jay got hurt, we had to lift him over the fence. He wasn't very happy about it.

I think the most lopsided scoring game we were ever involved in was when we played against another team, which included the James Brothers – Alan and Timmy. Well, during one particular play, Alan was tackled, and landed in a huge pile of fresh, steaming dog shit! It was smeared all over the back of his tee shirt, and he refused to take it off!!

I think he scored 15 touchdowns that day. Nobody wanted to tackle him!

There were miles of storm drains, which ran under the ball fields at Manchester High School. We used to walk deep into the catacombs, twisting and turning along this never-ending path, with only our flashlights to guide us, hoping that we didn't run into some beady little eyes staring back at us. Every once in a while we would stray from the main pipe system and crawl into one of the narrower tributary pipes. Until, one time while I was leading the way, with five or six of the guys behind me, we came up into a "room" which was covered with piles of rat shit. We screamed like a bunch of little girls, and got the hell out of there. I think that was the last time we went exploring there.

The guys used to like spending the night at my house, because my parents let us stay up. Normally, most of the gang were forced to go to bed by nine or ten o'clock, on the weekends. The only ones who got to stay up late on a regular basis were the Smith boys and me. So, Matt, Ryan and David were regular sleep over guests. We'd laugh ourselves sick, eat a lot of junk food and, every once in a while, we'd share some serious thoughts. These were few and far between, but I would be amazed when someone would offer up some esoteric, thought-provoking gem for us to ponder. Then someone would fart, and everything would be back to normal.

One time, Craig Haley set up a makeshift boxing ring in his front yard, and the testosterone started flowing, as Craig organized bout after bout, with some pretty vicious, yet funny results. AND, THE PARENTS DIDN'T STOP US FROM PUMMELLING EACH OTHER!

Craig had a match against Bob Dora, a tall, lanky kid who lived on Hollister Street. To this day, I do not know what would possess Bob to step in the ring with Craig. Either he was very brave or very stupid. The bell sounded, and Bob started dancing around the ring, bobbing and weaving, while throwing the occasional jab. Craig stood flat-footed, and followed Bob with his eyes. Someone from the crowd finally yelled out "Come on! Do something!" Bob lunged forward, and Craig hit him square in the eye with a right cross.

Bob's head snapped backed, and he was heard to mutter: "Nice punch!", as he slunk to the ground. One punch – over. Bob's eye swelled shut and turned red. It kinda looked like a baboon's ass.

Then, Mickey Callahan decided he wanted to box me. Now, Mickey was no physical specimen. Although he was a year older than me, he was smaller and weaker.

But, what he lacked in size and strength, he more than made up for with his mouth, his heart, his arrogance and, if he got mad, his uncontrollable insanity. Mickey truly believed that the extra year he had on this earth gave him an advantage over me, despite a history of run-ins where he always ended up with the short end of the stick. He never turned away from a fight.

The bell sounded. Mickey never landed one punch. I swarmed all over him, and hit him with about ten straight shots, knocking him through the hedges separating the Haley's yard from the Callahan's yard. Mickey went nuts and, with tears streaming down his cheeks and still wearing the boxing gloves, picked up a baseball bat, and chased me out of the neighborhood, screaming obscenities at me the whole way.

Of course, the rest of the gang was no help. They were too busy laughing.

Everybody carried a pocket knife; we all played with real-looking toy guns; we went all over town, and then some, and our parents never had to worry about us; we scraped our knees, bloodied our noses, lost teeth, broke bones, blackened eyes, bumped heads, got burned, got cut, got scarred, got mad, got sad, got even, cried, laughed, and had a blast. We were boys being boys...

...and, our parents never had to worry about us.

Chapter Nineteen
Sleep Habits

I don't know if there was something in the water, in Manchester, but it just seemed as if our gang had an inordinate number of weird sleep habits.

When I was around ten-years-old, I spent the night over the Haley's house. Why I thought this would be fun, was beyond me. Six kids in one household, and two long-suffering parents; why would I think this would be a good time? Moron!

So, here I am, in this rat hole of a room, shared by Craig, Ryan and Matt, which Mrs. Haley rightfully gave up trying to keep clean long ago. I mean, these guys were slobs, in the truest sense of the word. But, I digress...

I'm lying on the lower bunk of their bunk bed, just dozing off, after a hard day of play, when Ryan, who is sound asleep, starts singing "My country 'tis of thee, sweet land of liberty...", over and over and over. And, no form of shaking, yelling, or punching will bring him out of it.

While Ryan is on his 13th chorus of his patriotic ditty, Matt, who is on the upper bunk, and is also sound asleep, starts banging his head against his pillow – over and over and over.

"*My Country 'tis of thee…*"

(dooge, dooge, dooge…)

"*…sweet land of liberty…*"

(dooge, dooge, dooge…)

"*…of thee I siiiing…*"

(dooge, dooge, dooge…)

Now, I have never shared a room with anyone, being the only son. And, <u>this</u> is my first sleepover experience??? Screw this! I woke Mrs. Haley, and asked her to call my dad, to bring me home.

I did have another sleep encounter with Matt and Ryan, a couple of years later, when our moms took all the kids to Cape Cod, for a week of camping. The three of us shared a pop-up tent. You know, the ones that looked like an igloo? Anyway, our campsite was on a small hill, overlooking a lake. It was a perfect scene. We would play and swim all day, then go back to our campground by dusk, to eat our supper, like the pioneers we were. The moms loved it, because we were so worn out by the end of the day, we were no problem at all.

One night, in the wee hours, I woke up with a stabbing pain in my side. I soon realized that I was lying on something, and it was jabbing me in the ribs. Too tired to investigate the cause, I vainly tried to move away from the protrusion, only to be woken a short time later, having rolled back on top of it. This went on for most of the night, while Ryan and Matt were dead to the world. I was miserable. What made matters worse was that I couldn't seem to find the tent door. Apparently, Matt was sleeping in front of the door, and the zipper was buried beneath him. I was trapped, until morning,

Finally, mercifully, morning had come. I had squeaked out about three hours sleep the entire night, and was trying to catch a little more shuteye, when I was disturbed by a growing swell of laughter from outside our tent. What the hell was going on??? I gave up the thought of more sleep, and decided to find out what the commotion was about. The problem was that I couldn't find the door to the tent. And, why was the tent window on the ceiling??? I woke Ryan and Matt, so they could help me figure out what was going on. Why were we trapped???

We cleared away the sleeping bags, and found that we had been lying on the tent door. After a quick engineering conference, and some deft team work, we had managed to unzip the tent door, and maneuver our way out of our prison. That's when it dawned upon us – we had rolled the tent off of the campsite, down the hill, and had landed in the brush alongside a road. I had been lying on a tree stump. And, the laughter? Well, our camping neighbors from the surrounding sites had gathered to marvel at the unconscious work of three sleeping dummies. Did any of them offer to help us out? Nah! They were too busy staring and laughing. I think our moms were actually selling donuts and coffee.

I'm glad that my misery could bring such joy into your lives!

The Smith Boys were the Kings of Sleepwalking, hands down. And, I'm not just referring to stumbling and mumbling, I'm talking about full-blown theatrical productions, which have become legend.

The Smiths lived on Delmont Street, in a neat, little Cape Cod-style home. There were three bedrooms – the master bedroom, on the first floor, and two rooms upstairs. Larry, as the oldest, had his own room. Karl and Reese shared the room across the hallway.

One night, Karl was startled awake by a loud noise. He turned on the light, only to find Reese pulling toys and stuff from underneath his bed, and piling it in the center of the room. Karl just <u>had</u> to ask:

> *"Face! It's two o'clock in the morning! What the Hell are you doing???*
>
> *"Where is it, Karl?"*
>
> *"Where's what??"*
>
> *"My soda! What did you do with my soda???"*
>
> *"Idiot, go back to bed!"*

"I'm telling Mom!"

With that, Reese marched downstairs, while Karl and Larry were laughing hysterically. After several minutes, and no further conflict, Karl and Larry became curious as to what had happened to their dopey brother, and headed downstairs. There, in the bathroom, they found Reese, standing there, staring at his own feet. Why? To this day we don't know. Larry, taking on the role of concerned big brother, in his most caring, nurturing tone, exclaimed:

"Face! You big idiot! Go to bed!"

Another time, I showed up at their house, after work one night, and walked into their den, to find Reese sitting on the easy chair, watching television, and Karl lying on the couch. I simply said hello, and the strangest dialogue started:

"What's going on, Karl?"

"You remember Mark, who was in our math class?"

"Karl, I wasn't in your math class. You're two grades behind me."

"Bullshit! Don't lie! Mrs. Gowan was our teacher!"

"I'm telling you, we were never in class together!"

"Don't you remember the final exam?"

"I WASN'T IN CLASS WITH YOU!"

That's when it dawned on me – Karl was sound asleep! I let Reese in on the joke. He asked me if I was sure about that. I offered a demonstration:

"Karl, my ass itches. Does yours?"

"Yeah, it does!"

"Well, why don't you scratch it?"

"I'm too tired."

Of course, Reese and I laughed like hell.

The greatest sleepwalking "Shit On" occurred when Karl woke one night, to go to the restroom. He did his business, and went to bed. The only problem – in his half-sleeping stupor, he never made it downstairs to the bathroom. Instead, he walked into Larry's bedroom, and took a leak on top of his stereo.

The following morning, Larry woke up, and saw this puddle in the middle of his turntable dust cover. As the stereo was directly under an open window, Larry assumed it had rained the night before. He even stuck his hand in it, and sniffed!

To this day, I don't know if Karl ever fessed up.

George Hanson was probably the deepest sleeper. One time, while George was sound asleep in his own bed, Ken Hanson and Sid Orlowski picked up the mattress, and carried it and George out to the Hanson's pool deck, and left him there, until the next morning. When George finally woke up, he started freaking out, because he didn't know where he was.

Wear those emotional scars proudly, my friend!

Chapter Twenty
Corporal Punishment

This is truly a different era we live in. God forbid a parent would <u>ever</u> spank a child in public – the arrest would be shown on CNN, for the world to see – the parent's face would be broadcast on <u>America's Most Wanted</u>. Whatever happened to the old adage, "Spare the rod, spoil the child"? That's why there's a breakdown of morals and a gross lack of respect from today's kids – they're just not <u>scared</u> of their parents, anymore! Snot-nosed little bastards!

Not in <u>our</u> neighborhood, man! Corporal Punishment was a way of life, for all of us. Not a week would go by, that we didn't have a new story about one of the gang getting his ass turned red, by one of the parents. And, I'M TALKING ABOUT OUR MOMS! Not the dads - hell no! The threat of pissing Dad off was MUCH worse than what "Mom" could dole out – or, so we thought...

Most of the households had a "stay-at-home mom", who had to deal with their kids' stupidity on a day-to-day basis, while the dads had the sanctuary of their jobs.

And, we were good at pushing their buttons, until all hell broke loose.

True to form, my mom was the disciplinarian, in our house. Of course, like most kids, I had selective memory, never remembering what it felt like, from the last time I got my ass kicked. So, whenever I would mouth off, Mom would do the same routine – she would do an about-face, march into the living room, where she would find dad reading the newspaper, demand his leather belt right off of his waist, with a high-pitched "Ir-VING, GIVE me your BELT!" She would then commence chasing me around the house, to administer her unique brand of justice. What? You think any one of us were crazy enough to stand there, and take it?? Do you see "Stupid" written on my forehead?? (Don't answer that!)

And, when Mom caught you, it was always the same. It didn't matter <u>whose</u> mom it was; they all had the same beating technique:

"How…"

(whack!)

"Many…"

(whack!)

"Times…"

(whack!)

"do…"

(whack!)

"I…"

(whack!)

"have…"

(whack!)

"to…"

(whack!)

"tell…"

(whack!)

"you…"

(whack!)

"not…"

(whack!)

"to..."

(whack!)

"burp"

(whack!)

"the..."

(whack!)

"alphabet..."

(whack!)

The last time I ever got hit with a belt, I was about thirteen. I was in the kitchen, getting under Mom's skin, acting like a smart-mouthed little ass, when I pushed one button too many, and Mom went nuts!

She spun on her heels, into the living room: Ir-VING give me your BELT!"

I looked over my shoulder, to see Mom coming at me, with a full head of steam. I tried to run, but she was too fast. "Whap!" Right across my right arm. But, something was different, this time. It didn't hurt! For the first time, it didn't hurt! I had grown past the pain! I was six feet tall, and too tough for the belt!

With a newly-found sense of courage, and an arrogant attitude, I turned to Mom, and said: *"Try this arm!"* - pointing to my left. Mom was outraged! She reared back, and gave me a good one, "Whammo!" I just sneered. *"Try this one, again!"* Mom was "major pissed"!

> *"Again! Hit me again!"*

> *(Whap, whap whap!)*

I was feeling invincible for the first time in my life! Nothing could stop me, now! I was bigger and badder than my mother. I got right in her face, backing her up against the refrigerator:

> *"Is that the best you got??? Come on! Give me your best shot!*

And, in one fell swoop, she did. Mom turned the belt around, grabbed the buckle, and "Ga-DING", hit me in the middle of the forehead! I let out a wail, and started rolling around the floor, writhing in pain. Mom was stunned! She just dropped the belt, and ran to the living room, for a good cry.

When I regained my composure, I had come to the realization that I had gone way, way too far, this time. I made my mom cry – and the number one rule in kiddom was NEVER make your mom cry! I crawled into the living room, and begged her forgiveness. We hugged, and we resolved two things, that day – I was too big to spank, and I would never make my mom cry again. And, I didn't.

The buckle mark faded about six months later…

The funniest beating the gang was ever privileged to witness was the beating that Mrs. McNulty gave to her oldest son, Steve.

Now, it doesn't matter what the circumstances were, just suffice it to say that Steve mouthed off to Mrs. Mac, and the fun ensued. Steve ran out the front door, with Mom close behind, yelling "Steven! You get back here!" Steve kept running. While we're all standing on the street, egging them on, the two of them had lapped the outside of the house. Then, Steve ran in the front door, and up the stairs, and locked himself in his bedroom.

We could hear Mrs. Mac banging on the bedroom door, while yelling at her wayward son:

> *"Young Man! Open this door, this instant!"*

> *"No!"*

> *"Steven, I'm not going to warn you again! Open this door, right now, or I'm going to kick it in!"*

> *"Go ahead! I don't care!"*

That was it. The launch sequence was started. Steve had brought Mom to that magical place, where logic and calm leave the body of a normally-rational, caring, loving woman, transforming her into an uncontrollable she-beast, with one irrational thought on her mind – Kill the boy!

Mrs. Mac proceeded to kick out the bottom panel of the locked bedroom door, reached in, unlocked the door, flung it open, and started chasing Steve around the room. Steve made a mad dash down the stairs, and had thrown open the front door to make his great escape, when Mrs. Mac picked up the broken door panel, and winged it down the stairs, like a Frisbee, hitting Steve square in the back, sending him sprawling face-first to the sidewalk in front of his house, where he laid for several minutes, sobbing between attempts to catch his breath.

We, his loving, compassionate friends, laughed our asses off, enjoying someone else's misery. Mrs. McNulty just closed the door.

Now, THAT was a Kodak moment!

Chapter Twenty-One
Favorite Neighborhood Food

There were certain moms, who were known for certain food specialties - the ones that the gang would crawl over broken glass, to get a taste. We smell the heavenly aroma emanating from one of the kitchens, and we would <u>beg</u> to be invited to dinner.

Mrs. Haley made the best spaghetti on the block. We called it "Mama Haley's". Don't ask me why it's fair that an Irish mom could make such a great Italian dish – she just did. I considered it an honor to be invited to join them. One time, my Uncle John was invited to their house for a home-cooked spaghetti dinner. He and Mr. Haley were in the living room, talking, while Mrs. Haley was putting the food on the dining room table. She had left three pounds of cooked pasta in a serving dish, on the dining room table, and went back to the kitchen, to get the rest of the meal. When she returned ten minutes later, the pasta was gone – all three pounds of it! Come to find out that Ryan had snuck in, and devoured the entire bowl of pasta, leaving nothing for the rest of the family, or my uncle.

What a great guy!

Mrs. Corrado was responsible for preparing the greatest veal cutlets I would ever have, then or now. It also helped that Mr. Corrado was a meat cutter, and brought home the choicest meats. Anyway, when David would pack a lunch for school, or whatever, he would, inevitably, bring cutlet sandwiches. They were good as gold, as David could trade them for multiple desserts, or even money.

My mom, who would never be mistaken for a culinary expert, had the chili market cornered! She made the meatiest, three-bean chili around, and usually made a huge pot – enough for two or three meals. The Haley boys especially loved chili night. Even when they weren't invited for dinner, they would hang around at our back door, pressing their faces against the screen door, until mom would invite them in. Buncha moochers!

Mom would regularly invite the neighborhood kids over, to make homemade taffy, which would require the kids to coat their hands with butter, and join in, pulling and pulling this huge glob of hot, viscous sugar. When it began to harden, Mom would spread it out in long two-inch thick strands, on wax paper. When it eventually cooled, she would crack it with a knife, and send each kid home, with a huge chunk. I always thought she should mass-produce her recipe and sell it. It was that good!

The Watson family, who actually lived around the corner, on Hollister Street, used to grow and roast their own peanuts, once a year. They would then sell them around the neighborhood. A lot of allowance money was blown on this annual addiction.

The Orlowskis had their own grape vines, in their backyard. Every year, the gang would invade their yard, and stand under the arch of vines, and eat our fill, till our fingers and lips were purple.

Old Mrs. Chambers, who lived across the street from me, grew fresh rhubarb, in her garden. We would steal a bowl of sugar from my house, walk over to her garden, sit with our feet in the dirt, break off stalk after stalk, dip the ends in the sugar, and eat and eat and eat. Mrs. Chambers never minded. There was more than she could ever cook. She would see us there, and just wave.

Ahh! The simple pleasures of life.

Chapter Twenty-Two
Other Traditions

***1** : an inherited, established, or customary pattern of thought, action, or behavior (as a religious practice or a social custom) **2** : the handing down of information, beliefs, and customs by word of mouth or by example from one generation to another without written instruction*
- Webster's Dictionary

Like any small town, there were staples of tradition that brought the families together on a regular basis. Funny thing was, this was also true for me and my friends. There were events that were an annual "must do".

Parade watching was standard. Every Memorial Day and Independence Day, we would be at the corner of Summit and Center Streets, to watch the veterans, Boy and Girl Scouts, high school bands, and elected officials march or roll by. And, immediately following the parade, the guys would ride their bikes over to the American Legion Hall, where there were free hot dogs and hamburgers for the parade marchers. It didn't matter that our marching days were behind us; this is one tradition that we wouldn't let die.

Fourth of July fireworks were always held at Mt. Nebo, which wasn't a mountain in the true sense of the word. But, for years, it was the highest point in town which had road access. The families would sit on blankets on the ball field, and wait with great anticipation for the mayhem to begin. I can still feel the thump in my chest, as the bombs exploded overhead, close enough to where you felt as if you could almost touch them. The annual climax to the show included a tank war, where two ground displays, set at opposite ends of the field would fire roman candle shots at each other. This was high-tech for the sixties.

Summers were for the beach. My favorite was Misquamicut Beach, in Westerly, Rhode Island, which was about an hour and a half drive from our neighborhood. The best time was when it was overcast – the waves were always bigger. We would play all day, getting slammed around by the waves, digging a hole to China in the sand, eating salt water taffy, and crawling under the girls' bath house for a free show. You know, wholesome fun! Along the way, I would point out all the places where my sister Claudia puked from car sickness, on previous trips: *"Claud puked there, and there. And THAT one was particularly chunky!"*

One time, I went with the Hansons to East Beach, which was right down the road from Misquamicut, but a little less crowded. I wasn't in the water more than fifteen minutes, when a huge wave picked me up, and slammed me head first into the sand, almost knocking me unconscious. I dragged myself to the beach, crawled to the blanket, and passed out for much of the day, not waking up until it was time to go home. This was a source of great humor to my loving, caring friends. And, to this day, they have never let me forget that – bastards!

My dad would always load the family, and two or three of the neighborhood kids into the station wagon, and trek us up there. Along the way, he would always threaten to turn the car around and go home, either due to the noise or the smells emanating from the back seat. He never did, though…

We had an above-ground swimming pool. We were the only ones who had a pool, until the Hansons got a deck pool a few years later. Anyway, the tradition was that, every summer, despite how anyone felt about me in the neighborhood, I became everyone's best friend. It only made sense. It was a lot easier to stay cool in the Manns' pool instead of having to peddle your bike across town. Dad used an old picnic table to build a huge diving platform, which we took full advantage of. Throw in a couple of truck tire inner tubes, and let the ass-breakers begin! Burt Stewart did the biggest belly flops in the area. When he hit the water, the level would drop six inches. He was cool.

Riverside Park was an amusement park in Agawam, Massachusetts, which was about ninety minutes from Manchester. Every Spring, the local airwaves would be inundated with their familiar commercial: "Take Route 91 to a world of fun – Riverside Park!" And, we did, year after year.

It was your typical amusement park, with bumper cars, midway games, tunnel of love, fried cinnamon dough, cotton candy, and the biggest, baddest, OLDEST wooden roller coaster on the eastern seaboard – The

Thunderbolt. It rattled, it creaked, and it scared the hell out of us. We loved it. One day, The Haleys and the Manns drove up there for the day, and it rained most of the early morning. When the skies cleared at around 10:00 AM, there was virtually no one in the park, but us. Ryan, Matt and I went to the Thunderbolt, and rode it continuously, for eighteen rides – just the three of us. What a great day!

We used to go to Riverside on Friday nights for the stock car races. The two coolest events at the race track were the figure eight races and of course, demolition derbies. One time, a particularly hot and humid Friday night, I went to the races with Jason Parrett, another kid from the neighborhood. We ate all the prerequisite food, at the races, and decided to go on some rides. The first ride was Tilt-a-Whirl. That's the one where two people sit in what looks like a ski lift seat, which has an umbrella-like canopy above. As the ride progresses, the center arm of the ride raises, while the passengers are swept in a circle low to high, over and over and over and over…

Well, fried dough greasy pizza, hot weather and centrifugal force did not bode well for me. I was getting nauseous. I pleaded with the ride operator to stop the ride, and let me off. He refused. I imagined him standing there, with a maniacal grin on his face, snickering at my predicament. Again, I yelled for the ride to stop, but got nothing. I tried, but I couldn't hold back! I leaned over the side of the carriage, opened wide and, like a machine gun in an old army movie, wiped out half of the moms, dads and kids waiting in line for the ride – including the ride operator. Screams of terror and disgust were rampant. When the ride finally stopped, Jay and I walked toward the exit. The operator of the ride glared at us, and asked in one of us got sick on the ride. Jay and I looked at each other, and replied: "Nope! Not us!"

Every Fall, it was never too difficult for our parents to get their leaves raked, for one reason and one reason only –we got to burn the leaves! A bunch of us would go to each other's yards, rake up every leaf we could find into one huge pile, and light that sucker on fire! And, this was acceptable to our parents! The bigger the pile, the bigger the fire, the bigger the maniacal smiles on our faces.

Of course, as usual, all good things must come to an end, as leaf burning was outlawed in the early seventies – some bullshit about the environment and pollution...

Every Thanksgiving morning, regardless of the weather, we would be back on the same corner, watching the Manchester Turkey Day Race. Believe it or not, this race is internationally known, and runners come from all over the world to compete. We would cheer on the competitors, and yell at the people we knew. It was always a special moment when someone would puke while running. Always good for a laugh! To this day, whenever any of us are in town during one of these events, it's an unwritten rule that we meet on that corner, knowing that one or more of our gang would be there.

Then, it was on to the Thanksgiving Day football game, between cross-town rivals Manchester High and East Catholic. Then, we'd all go home for dinner.

Two weeks prior to Christmas, those of us who had paper routes (Karl, Larry, Ted, David and I) would hand out the annual holiday cards to each of our customers, in search of the customary holiday tip. This was a very lucrative time for us. We would each do our subscription collections the week before the holiday, and rake in what, to us, was a lot of money. On average, each of us collected anywhere from $100 to $250.00, which was a huge score for us. That would buy some decent Christmas presents. The one thing I never understood, were the "stiffs" who ignored the fact that we busted our asses for an entire year, rain or shine, to deliver their papers to them. And, they didn't think that had any value. Funny, but they were always the first to complain when their paper got soaked or blew away, which could happen more frequently for them.

Christmas morning, after the presents were opened, the wrapping paper cleared, and breakfast done, the gang would all meet on Delmont Street to compare notes:

>"What you get?"

>"I got a Hot Wheels track!"

>"I got a new bike!"

>"I got a bat and glove!"

>"I got socks!"

Clothes always sucked, for a Christmas present.

The Haley brothers were good about smashing their stuff before they ever got to report on it. By the time the trash was put out for weekly collection, there would be some Christmas gift that had met an untimely fate, hours after it's unveiling. I know it must have driven their parents mad. Again, I can hear the impassioned wail of "Matt, stop being a mental!"

Every New Year's Eve, it was understood that we all would listen to WDRC radio, to hear the Top 100 Countdown, of the top songs of the year, the last of which would play just before midnight, and the New Year. Karl and I even spent one night at Bentley School, listening to the show on my transistor radio, while playing on the swing set, jumping off to see who could fly further into a pile of snow.

Board games were huge, in our neighborhood. Risk games would on for two or three days. We'd leave the board in its place, go home to sleep, get up the next day, and pick up where we left off. Monopoly and backgammon were also big. So was Strat-O-Matic Baseball, which was a dice game which used Major

League Baseball Players' statistics from the previous year. Every year, Teddy would buy the newest version and, of course, claim the Red Sox before anyone else had a chance. Larry would take the Yankees, Ken took the Reds, George took the Cubs. I usually played the Oakland A's.

We played a lot of cards – sometimes poker but, more times than not, the game was Setback, This was a game that could be played either as singles or teams. The object was to get high, low, jack and game of the same suit. We played for hours. There was one time that we had to end early, though. Karl had terrible gas, and John Graff, another buddy from another neighborhood, threatened to leave if Karl cut one more fart. Well, Karl was up to <u>that</u> challenge, and John stormed out, while the rest of us convulsed with laughter. What a bunch of intellectuals!

In the early seventies, the United Artists Theaters East opened at the Manchester Parkade. The theater would eventually put the State Theater out of business, because it was new, clean, and had 2 theaters, showing two different double features. But, the biggest attraction to me, and the rest of the gang, was the Midnight

Movies at the "UA". Every Friday and Saturday night, at midnight, movies were shown, usually a double feature, until the wee hours of the morning. A bunch of us would get together to walk from the neighborhood, to the theater, which was about two miles away, and our parents actually let us go! We would join hundreds of other young teens to watch some piece of crap, low-budget horror movie, or some other highly-Educational fare, such as <u>Reefer Madness</u>. The fun part was trying to bust everyone up by yelling out snappy retorts during the movie. As the night wore on, the audience would become increasingly quiet. Eventually, looking around you would see most of the audience sound asleep. It was a long walk home at four or five in the morning.

For years, everyone in town would go the Manchester Drive-In, which was actually located in Bolton Notch, on the border shared with Bolton. It was your typical drive-in, with a playground, where the kids would play before the movie, tinny sound emanating from six hundred car speakers, mosquitoes the size of sparrows, and the corny commercials for the snack bar, with the dancing boxes of popcorn, acrobatic hot dogs, and the bad actors, touting all the "mouth-watering treats" available.

And, the commercials LIED! "Pizza! None better anywhere (worse than frozen)", "Fresh, buttered popcorn" (came in huge plastic bags, pre-popped, and warmed under heat lamps). But, we ate it, because it was there.

It was the place for families, indigestion, mosquito bites, dirty PJ's, young love, and steamed-up windows. It's gone, now – another victim of progress. But, the memories will last forever.

I had my own traditions that I never shared with anyone, never told anyone about. Every winter, from the age of eight, during the first snowfall of the year, I would sneak out of the house in the middle of the night, and walk up to the cow pasture at the end of Delmont Street, sit under one of the oak trees at the top of the hill, and just listen to the snow fall. You know, when it's absolutely quiet, and all you hear is the "shhhhhhh" sound, as the flakes hit the ground. It brought a complete sense of peace to me.

I got the same satisfaction from walking in the drizzling rain – nothing too heavy – just enough to hear the sound of car tires going by, and sail a popsicle stick boat down the street gutter.

During the summers, the New England area would have several thunder storms – a good, stiff rain, and lots of lightning and crashing thunder. This was always my cue to go into our basement, open the windows, and lie on the couch, just to listen to the myriad of noises and emanating from the storm. I would always drift off to sleep.

Do you see a trend, here?

Chapter Twenty-Three
The "Skip" Day

Larry was in ninth grade; I was in eighth. We decided to skip school.

The plan was to spend the day at Larry's house and, basically, do whatever the hell we wanted. Since his mom was at work, we didn't worry about any of the parents finding out, as long as we kept it low key, and didn't run around outside, until school was over, for the day.

I left my house that morning, and walked around the corner to the Smith's, and opened the back door, only to meet Karl as he was leaving for school.

> *"What are you doing here?'*
>
> *"Larry and I are skipping school, today."*
>
> *"Really? I think I'll skip school, too."*

Great idea! A short while later, Dwight Gilman, who lived on the other end of Delmont Street, showed up to walk with Karl, to school. When he learned that we were all playing "hooky", he decided to join us. ANOTHER great idea!

The only problem – when the sixth grade teacher at Bentley School took student roll call, and Dwight wasn't there, everyone became concerned, because he was seen walking to school that morning. The teacher informed the principal, and the principal called Dwight's mom.

Dwight's mom, knowing that Dwight was going to pick Karl up, showed up at the Smith's front door:

>"Oh shit! Dwight's mom is here!"

>"Karl, go answer the door!"

>"Why should I answer it?"

>"Because, Moron, it's obvious that someone squealed on Dwight, and he wouldn't be coming over to see anybody but you!"

Karl opened the door, and Dwight was busted. Mrs. Gilman took him to school to face the music. Karl was now in panic mode. He knew Dwight would crack, and would give Karl up. Larry and I tried to calm Karl down. We told him that he couldn't be sure that Dwight would say anything…

…then, the phone rang.

> "Karl, answer the phone."
>
> "Why should I answer it?"
>
> "Because, Shit for Brains, nobody else would be calling here during the day, unless it was for you."
>
> "What makes you think it's for me?"
>
> "Call it an Educated guess!"

Karl answered the phone. It was Mrs. Woods, the Principal of Bentley School. Dwight gave him up. Mrs. Woods wanted Karl to report to school immediately, if not sooner. He grabbed his coat, and left, unsure of his fate. It was just Larry and I, now.

We wondered if anything would happen to us. Would Karl be forced drop the dime on Larry and me? Nah! We convinced ourselves that he would keep our secret.

As it turned out, Larry would be caught without anyone's help. He was required to bring an absentee note from his mom in order to get back in school. Of course, that wasn't about to happen. He was given a week's detention, and his mom was informed of his truancy.

Karl and Dwight were also given a week's detention. But, they had attained legendary status around the halls of Bentley School. They skipped school. They were bad boys. They were cool.

I got away with it, by sweet-talking the school nurse at Illing Junior High. I also needed a note, but told her that I forgot to get it. I promised to bring it the following day. I never did.

Some of us are born under a lucky star, or are just better bullshitters that most. Take your pick.

Chapter Twenty-Four
The Draft

I was twelve years old, when I started delivering newspapers. That was 1969. The Vietnam War was in full swing, and thousands of young men were losing their lives or coming home in pieces, either physically or mentally. The draft lottery was reinstated that same year to fill shortages left by dwindling volunteers. Face it, this war was losing popularity, and the draft was the only way to get new blood.

One of my stops on my paper route was this huge Victorian house, on North Elm Street. It was, for lack of a better description, an unofficial fraternity house for Manchester Community College, as most of the ten or twelve guys who lived there were attending school there. The others were just glad to be out of their parents' homes. This was a cool place to hang out, as there was a party there almost every weekend, and the guys were cool about letting me hang out, I guess I was kind of like their mascot.

Although everybody seemed to get along, there was definitely some mistrust among them. They had five separate refrigerators in the kitchen, three of which were padlocked. And, I delivered four papers to the house! Ahh, thievery! Bad for them, good for me!

It was Wednesday, July 1st, 1970. I had just arrived at the "Frat House" to make the daily delivery. As usual, I walked in the back door, into the kitchen. I immediately noticed that the house was eerily quiet. Usually, there would be all kinds of activity going on. How could there not be, with 12 guys and their friends coming in and out at all hours; but, not on this day.

I walked through the kitchen, down the hallway, and into the living room. There, huddled around a nineteen-inch black and white television, were several incredibly nervous draft-age young men transfixed by the draft lottery. There they were, watching their future being determined by a couple of old farts pulling a pill out of a drum, which contained a fateful date – a date which could mean life or death to some of them.

I unobtrusively sat on the arm of a couch, and just observed the drama which was playing out around me.

This entire scenario seemed surreal to me. Up to this point, I hadn't really given the war much thought. What the heck did I know about Vietnam? I was 12. It didn't affect me. But now, there were people I knew who were facing their collective futures. And, one or more of them may not be here, for long. I didn't like the feeling. I hadn't experienced death of someone who was close to my age. Vietnam was so far away, and didn't or shouldn't affect Manchester or anyone in my little, safe and secure life.

Soon, the lottery was drawing to a close. You could hear the proverbial pin drop. When the last number was drawn and announced, the silence exploded into screaming and yelling and hugging and high fives. Not one of my older friends had been drafted – not one. They literally dodged a huge bullet.

There was a <u>huge</u> party that night.

Chapter Twenty-Five
Fellow Mentals at Illing

To be expected, Teddy Hanson and I ended up going through Illing Junior High School together, where we shared several classes. I don't know if the school administrators planned this, but we found ourselves in classes with an inordinate number of "class clowns". It was as if they had decided it was better to keep us all together, to minimize the damage. There was no better example of this, than Mrs. Velte's eighth grade history class.

Mrs. Velte was old – very old, by teaching standards. I'm guessing that she was pushing 70. But, what did we know? At 14, every adult looks like they're ancient. She was a short woman, about 5' 4" tall, with the patience of Job. And, we put her to the test, constantly.

Besides Teddy and myself, there was John Graff, Dave Yankowski, Dan Bossy, Sam Turkleton, and too many other demented characters to list here, all with a "can you top this?" attitude, where the goal was to crack everyone else up, and gain the unofficial title of "King of Class Clowns".

Mrs. Velte was easy to fool. Whenever anyone wanted to get out of class, they would tell me. Why? I had a knack for impersonating the vice principal's voice over the intercom system in the classroom. I would imitate the prerequisite pops and clicks which were heard whenever the intercom was about to interrupt the class, then request that Mrs. Velte to send a particular student down to his office. It worked every time. I usually used it for my own "skips". One time, I pulled off a quadruple, when "the voice on the intercom" requested that Teddy, Dave, Dan and I all come to the office. Mrs. Velte glared at us, sternly asking "What did you boys do???"

We went down to the gym, to play basketball.

Mrs. Velte was saddled with the duty of showing the drug prevention filmstrips mandated by our Board of Education. If you've forgotten how they worked, this was pre-video tape. Each series of film strips came with a corresponding set of 33 RPM record albums, which had intermittent "beeps", prompting you to feed the next slide into place. As each class had members of the Audio

Visual Club assigned to run all film projectors, Teddy and I were assigned to Mrs Velte. Kinda like giving matches and dynamite to a monkey, huh?

Well, far be it for us to ever pass up an opportunity. So, for the next few days, the projector was slightly out of focus, the record was slightly too soft to hear, and the theme music caused the entire class to lose their collective minds, as we sarcastically kept beat with that "cool" theme song.

Mr. Cox, our science teacher, had to teach the boys about sex Education. And, back then, then school board would show us a "how to" movie, complete with animated scenes of the "act". As you can imagine, this was a source of uncontrollable snickering and stifled laughter, as Dan Bossy is adding his own form of commentary: "Wow! Do they _really_ do that?" "Why is it pointing up like that?" "Why do they call it a boner?".

Lester Fox was one of the few African-American students in the school, and he was appropriately cool. He dressed cool, he walked cool, and spoke very few words, which was cool!

One thing that was uniquely Lester's was his salute to the "Cafeteria Gods". See, since each class was brought to the cafeteria at the same time every day, Lester ended up at our table, more times than not. We always sat at a table right under the clock on the wall. And, every day, Les would buy an ice cream bar with the hard chocolate coating. And, whenever anyone would drop a lunch tray, thus distracting the teachers who were monitoring our activities, Les would take this opportunity to throw his ice cream at the clock. The teachers would return to their posts, only to find Lester's mess dripping down the wall. Don't ask me why, but it was funny as hell.

On the last day of school of our eighth grade year, Dan Bossy is walking out of the cafeteria with his used lunch tray, when he turns to Ryan Haley and says "Trip me!" Of course, Ryan was glad to oblige, and stuck out his foot. Dan, in most-dramatic fashion, flung his tray, dishes and all, about ten feet in the air. The entire student body, on hand to witness this act, collectively sucked the air out of the room, as the tray seemed to rise in slow motion and spin in suspended animation, finally crashing to earth in a shower of porcelain, utensils and uneaten green beans. A resounding "yyyyyyaaaaAAAAAAYYYYY!" rang throughout the cafeteria, while a "SPLAT" emanated from the clock.

It was a proper finish to another school year.

Although we all had our moments of brilliance, there was, without a doubt, one genius who stood out above the rest; an "artist" who took classroom chicanery to a new level, who inspired us all to reach for the stars and to achieve our own place in the annals Class Clown history. His name was Donald Taylor.

Don was a slightly built, mousy little guy, with horn-rimmed glasses, and long hair, who was an extremely intelligent, well-read chess player, who was into reading fantasy, horror, and Conan the Barbarian books, while listening to Black Sabbath records. He was truly a renaissance man, with an incredibly warped sense of humor.

Case in point, while in English class, we were assigned an oral book report, which we would read to the rest of the class. Mrs. Welch, our English teacher, was a complete and utter BITCH, who never had a nice thing to say about any of her students, told us that we could choose any book we wanted to, to complete the assignment. Don, in his infinite wisdom, chose to report on <u>Everything you Wanted to Know About Sex, But Were Afraid to Ask</u>, complete with graphic highlights from some of the more interesting chapters. We were dying! Here's Don, standing in front of the class, absolutely straight-faced, enlightening the entire class about Spanish Fly, rim jobs and the joys of a good three-way! Mrs. Welch lost her mind! She threw him out of class, amidst our thunderous applause, flunked him on the paper, and demanded that he return to school with his parents.

His mom came to school with Don, and they met with the vice principal and Mrs. Welch, to determine Don's fate. Mrs. Taylor came to her son's defense, stating that, although Don hadn't chosen the most appropriate material for his report, he <u>did</u> follow directions, by making his own choice for the report. It was agreed, between the grown-ups that Donald would write a new report, in place of his first report. Don refused. He held his ground, and kept his integrity intact. He had written his report, completed his assignment, and fulfilled his responsibility to Mrs. Welch. He would not be censored! Now, it was a matter of pride and principle!

He was suspended for a week, but never did re-write the report. What balls he had!

Don and I ended up hanging around through junior high. He introduced me to Black Sabbath, Alice Cooper, Conan the Barbarian, H.P. Lovecraft, J.R.R. Tolkein, and all-night chess tournaments. He was, truly one of the most intellectual friends I had. We eventually drifted apart in high school, though, as Don really got into the drug scene, and I couldn't go there. One time, in high school, Don came up to me in the cafeteria, stoned as hell, and said: *"You know Mann, you're so straight! One of these days, I'm gonna drop a hit of acid in your milk!"* And, he was laughing!

I looked him right in his bloodshot eyes, and said: *"You'd better hope it kills me! Because, when I come down, I'm gonna fucking <u>kill</u> you!"*

That was the last time I saw Don, for the rest of high school.

I ran into Don several years later, at one of our high school reunions, and he was a born-again Christian. He was still funny, still intelligent, married with children, with no residual effects from years of drug abuse. The only problem was that he had absolutely no memory of high school, at all. All he remembered was our short friendship at Illing Junior High.

Just say "No", kids!

Chapter Twenty-Six
Spring Thaw

I had mentioned the blue, plastic boats in a previous chapter. They came into play on another occasion, and almost got me arrested.

One winter, we had a particularly early spring thaw, and everything was pretty darned soggy. One of the families in our neighborhood was the Brummels. They had a very unique backyard, the surrounding yards were all higher than theirs. So, when the thaw came, there was about three feet of water in their backyard.

Of course, we were absolutely unable to pass up this opportunity. One night, Larry, Karl, David and I grabbed a couple of boats, and carried them down the street to our newly-formed inland lake, and decided to take a little sail.

I decided to go first. I placed the boat in the water, stepped in, and the guys pushed me away from shore. I was about two minutes into this inaugural voyage, when the backyard floodlights came on, illuminating the entire yard. And, of course, the guys scrambled for cover, leaving me to fend for myself.

Mrs. Brummel walked out on her back porch, and immediately demanded that I leave her property.

> *"I will, as soon as the tide comes in!"*
>
> *"If you don't leave right now, I'm going to call the police!"*
>
> *"And tell them what? There's someone sailing in your backyard?"*

The guys were laughing hysterically. Mrs. Brummel stormed into the house, and slammed the door. I figured that I had better get going while the getting was good.

No, the cops never showed up. I think Mrs. Brummel was too embarrassed to call them.

I had mentioned that we grew up with a swimming pool in the backyard. It was an above-ground model, which was approximately five feet deep, complete with a diving platform that Dad had constructed out of our old picnic table, and two-by-fours. We never took the pool down. It would freeze over every winter, thaw out every spring, and be ready by the time the hot weather set in. It provided years of fun, and ensured that I was going to be the most-popular kid in the neighborhood, at least for a few weeks every summer.

I was about 15, when I awoke one Sunday morning in early March, at about 7:30. It was raining pretty heavily, which signaled that spring was on the way. I was standing at the kitchen sink, drinking a glass of water, and daydreaming out the window, when I heard a rumble.

I looked toward the swimming pool when it happened. With a huge roar, the side of the pool just exploded, sending a monstrous tidal wave of water and ice, cascading into the yard below, slamming our neighbor's German Shepherd into the back of its owner's house! I remember the poor dog howling in fear, as it stood on the back porch, shivering.

It was the end of an era. We were all getting older, and busier, and the pool was slowly being forgotten for bigger adventures. But, for about ten years, it was our fair weather friend.

Chapter Twenty-Seven
The Day Things Changed Forever

I had a bad nightmare, in early 1972. I dreamt that I was in a funeral home, kneeling in front of a closed casket. It was two-tone blue, with antiqued silver handles. On the lid were several floral arrangements, and an 8x10 framed photo of Freddy Corrado. I remember turning around to see all the friends and extended family sitting in the wake room, in very specific places. David, "Doctor Bob" and Mrs. Corrado, and their daughters, were sitting to my right.

Then, I woke up.

I told David about my dream, the next morning. I remember David saying *"That's pretty weird",* and nothing more was said. We just forgot about it. Several months passed.

It was Saturday, August 19, 1972.

My dad, David and I drove to Springfield, Massachusetts to see the World Wrestling Federation. The matches started at 8:00 PM, and continued till about 10:30. We had ringside seats, and were hoarse from yelling and screaming throughout the course of the evening. My dad took us for bite to eat on the way home, and we didn't get back until after 1:00 AM. We dropped David off, in front of his house, and arrived at our house, about three minutes later. I washed up, and went straight to bed.

The following morning, I guess it was around 10:00, Claudia came busting in my bedroom. She had been crying. "Go find David!", she sobbed. I was pissed off that she woke me up. "Why?", I said in my grumpiest big brother tone. Through her sobs, Claudia blurted out – "Freddy's dead!"

I catapulted out of bed and backed my sister against the bedroom door:

"You're a damned liar!"

"No! Really! He was hit by a car last night! David took off, and nobody knows where he is!"

I ran down the stairs, bolted out the front door, and ran to the corner, in a vain attempt to find David. I was still in my pajamas. It was then that Tommy Dora, another neighborhood kid, rode up on his bike:

"Eric, what the hell are you doing?"

"Go find David! Freddy's dead, and David took off! Nobody knows where!"

Tommy took off like a shot, not knowing where to look, only knowing he had to try. By the time I got back to my house, Mom told me that David was home – that he was in Mr. Hirsch's cellar, next door, where Mr. Hirsch was trying to calm him down. I got dressed, and ran over there.

David was standing in his garage. When he saw me walking up the driveway, the floodgates opened. We hugged and cried for a long time. It seemed that Freddy, who worked at a local gas station, went to pick up his paycheck. While there, a tow truck call came in – there was a breakdown on the highway, and Freddy's friend and co-worker, Mel Goodwill, was leaving to do the tow. He asked Freddy to join him, and Freddy accepted. When they arrived at the scene, Mel and Freddy hopped out of the truck, and greeted the owner of the disabled car. Mel went to work, hooking up the car, while Freddy and the owner walked toward the front of the vehicle, to see if there was an easy fix to the problem. But, they made a fatal mistake. They walked around the left side of the car, near the traffic lane, instead of on the right side, on the shoulder of the highway.

It was at that exact moment that a drunk driver swerved into their lane, and killed Freddy and the car owner, instantly.

David was irrationally blaming himself for not being home when it happened. I assured him that he had no way of knowing, and that he couldn't have prevented it, anyway.

I ended up spending the better part of the next few days at David's house, running errands for the family – things like that. Mrs. Corrado barely left her bedroom, until the day of the wake.

Holmes Funeral Home, on Main Street, handled the funeral arrangements. On the day of the wake, I drove there with David and his family. When we entered the building, dozens of mourners had already arrived, with many more were to follow. I stayed in the lobby, while the Corrados met with the funeral director, and prepared to start the wake. The place filled to capacity. It seemed as if every family in the neighborhood was represented. Add to that the aunts, uncles and cousins of the Corrado family, and it was standing room only. Strange thing, though, none of the "gang" was there.

When the wake started, people started lining up to pay their respects, and say a prayer for Freddy.

I finally got in line. When I made it to the front of the line, I kneeled in front of the casket, for a moment of prayer. That's when my blood ran cold. There, in front of me, was a two-tone blue casket, with antiqued silver handles. On the lid were several floral arrangements, and an 8x10 framed photo of Freddy – placed exactly as in my dream! I was in shock! I turned around to look at the mourners in the room, and everyone was in the exact place they were sitting in my dream. I slowly turned my head toward David, who was sitting with his family, elbows on his knees, staring at the floor. When he finally looked up, and saw the stunned look on my face, it took him a few seconds to realize what was going on. Then, it hit him. His jaw dropped open, he pointed a finger at me, and blurted out *"You knew!"*

That was too much for me to handle. I lost it. I immediately left the room, went outside, and just sobbed. Shortly, David followed after me. He was simply amazed. *"You knew this was going to happen! How the hell did you know?"*

I struggled for an answer: *"I don't know. Every once in a while I do that. The only problem is I never know exactly <u>when</u> it's going to happen."*

I felt helpless; as if there was anything I could have done to prevent this tragedy. David and I talked about it for a while and, I think that's when we both came to the conclusion that there nothing any of us could have done. Each of us is destined to die on a particular day, of a particular year, at a particular time, and nothing we do will ever change that.

When I had composed myself, we returned to the wake room. But, where was the "gang"?

That question would be answered a short time later, when the double doors leading to the room opened, and in marched all the guys from the neighborhood, from oldest to youngest – with Craig Haley in the front, to Matt Haley in the rear; every one of them. This was their tribute to Freddy. This was their moment of solidarity. No more kid stuff; no more petty squabbles; that didn't matter anymore. There wasn't a dry eye in the house. It was truly a beautiful moment. David and his family loved it.

Freddy was buried the next day.

We lost one of our own, and life would never be the same. We were older that day, hardened, more appreciative of what we had. I truly do not recall another disagreement or fight among the gang, from that day, forward. It seemed that, without ever coming out and saying it, we grew closer. We grew up.

Chapter Twenty-Eight
Cars

Larry, Me, Teddy, David, Karl – That was the order in which we each got our driver's licenses. It was based upon when each of us turned sixteen years old. Of course, it was a monumental rite of passage, so none of us were going to let our parents delay the inevitable. Gas was cheap, and we could drive on a couple of bucks.

In most cases, each of us was stuck driving our parents' cars, until we saved up enough to buy our own. In my case, I usually drove my mom's 1967 American Motors Rebel. It was a two-door sedan with a black vinyl roof, black cloth interior, and a piss yellow paint job, and Nash seats - you know the seats that fold down to make a bed? Well, the driver's seat latch was defective and the seat would intermittently fold down, without warning, causing the driver to panic *("Put the Seat back! Put the seat back!")*, and the passengers to laugh like hell. Although it wasn't the greatest car, it was always accessible to me, as mom went to work in a car pool every day. So, more times than not, I would drive the guys down to Dairy Queen for lunch, during school. And, we were not always the most responsible individuals on the road.

It was about this time that Ringo Starr had released his single "Oh My My", which became our anthem, and we loved it. It had a driving beat, with a beer hall feel, and we would all act like total whackos when it came on the radio, swinging our arms back and forth, singing badly at the top of our lungs, and generally drawing attention to ourselves. But, we didn't care.

Every day, on Middle Turnpike, there was a crazy woman who used to stand on the sidewalk in front of her house, scribbling down the license plate numbers of random cars that would go by. She would then take those numbers to the local police station to report her findings. The police just humored her.

Of course, we couldn't let this opportunity go by. More times than not, while driving by her, whomever happened to be sitting in the front passenger seat would steer the car, while I would lean as far out of the window as I could, and let out a huge "Crockett Cry", causing our demented victim to write furiously in her little notebook. I always wondered how she explained that one to the cops.

During these lunchtime trips, a staple of Teddy's arsenal was to wait until there were three of us in the front seat, let's say me driving, Karl in the middle, and Teddy in the passenger seat. Teddy would choose this moment to wait until we drove by people we knew, reach over, honk the car horn, and duck down, so it would look like Karl and I would be cuddling. He would then yell, at the top of his lungs, *"Hey! Look at this cute couple!* He just got a huge kick out of this. Frankly, I just think he liked the idea of ducking down, with his head in Karl's lap! Ahhhhhhhh, Shit on!

I finally lost that car. How I lost it remains a particularly sore spot, to this day. Karl and I were coming home from taking Mom's car to an auto mechanic, and we were coming down Hollister Street. I approached the corner at Clifton Street, which was a blind corner, and turned left. There, as usual, parked no less than three feet from the curb, was Fat Gordy Gallasso's Oldsmobile Sedan. I swerved to miss it, but it was too late. My right front fender, hit Gordy's left rear fender, and just CRUNCHED Mom's car. It barely put a dent on Gordy's fender.

I did the right thing. I got out of the car walked up to the Gallasso's front door, and knocked, and knocked, and knocked. There was no answer. Since I knew I would have to report this accident. I parked my car behind his, turned it off, and Karl and I walked around the corner to call the police, to file a report. We then immediately walked back to the scene of the accident, and Gordy was waiting. He had moved his car closer to the curb, knowing he would be held partially liable, otherwise. I confronted him with this fact, and he blatantly denied moving the car, although Karl and I were both argued this point to the cop. The cop told me that there wasn't any proof, and that I would be liable.

Gordy's fender dent? About the size of a half dollar – an easy fix. Not with Gordy! That fat bastard presented my dad with a repair bill for $800.00! Dad told him he was full of shit; that there was no way it would cost that much. Gordy wouldn't take no for an answer. He submitted that bill to my insurance company, and they paid it! That was a lot of money back then, and for him to stick to one of his neighbors like that? Well, suffice it to say that payback is and <u>was</u> a bitch, over the next few years. But, I won't go there, on the grounds that it may incriminate me.

Mom's car was totaled. It was towed away to the junkyard. It was as if a friend had died. Rest in peace.

Dad drove a 1973 power blue Pontiac Catalina. What a land tuna! It had a huge eight cylinder engine, and could have slept a family of five.

Larry's first car was a Ford Pinto. You know, the one that exploded when it was rear ended? He hated that car, but his grandfather talked him into buying it. He would later trade it in for a beautiful Pontiac Firebird, with the huge, black firebird decal on the hood.

Ted always had nice cars. My favorite was a 1970 Dodge Challenger, light blue, with black top and interior.- a true muscle car. Gorgeous. He then traded that in for a black Camaro. Nothing but the best for Teddy!

David had a sleek Chrysler Convertible, which he inherited from his dad. I loved that car. It was a great cruising machine. I don't know why he ever got rid of it.

My first car? A 1965 Ford Custom, which I bought for $150. It was nothing special, but I liked it. That is, until I got rear-ended by a high school chum, on a rainy road, and snapped the frame, totaling the car. I sold it to the Manchester Volunteer Fire Department for $25.00, and they burned it up during one of their training drills.

The next car I bought was a 1959 Chevy Impala Convertible – you know, the Batmobile? It had a 283cc engine and a Hurst shifter. I kept that car until I moved to California, after college. The guy I sold it to blew the engine in the first week. What a douche!

Every week, my phone would ring off of the hook, with the guys calling up to bum rides to the Teen Center, which was on top of the Nike Site Ski slope, on the south end of town. It was run by the Recreation and Parks Department, and a different band played every week.

One time, Ted, Karl, David, my girlfriend Sue and I were heading up to the Teen Center, and the guys wanted to stop at the bottom of the slope, on the dark dead end road, to drink some beer. I was the designated driver. David and Karl were in the back seat, and Ted, Sue and

I were in the front. The guys were drinking their beers and tossing the bottles into the woods on the side of the road. When they were finished, I started the car, and proceeded toward to Teen Center.

All of a sudden, a set of headlights was coming down the road, directly at me. I got a bad feeling about this, so I stopped the car, and waited for the oncoming car to pass. When the headlights were right on top of us, the offending car pulled around to the side of us. I didn't hesitate, and hit the gas, determined to get the hell out of there. That's when I looked in the rear view mirror, and saw the "gumball" light up on top of the car. I could only muster two words: "Oh shit!'

David started freaking out: "Stop the car! Let me out! My dad's gonna kill me.

I yelled back: "Shut the hell up! You're not getting out! You're in this like the rest of us!" The cop car pulled right behind us, and I pulled over, immediately. The officer got out of his car, and marched up to my window. He was none too happy:

> *"You know I could arrest you right now, for running from me!"*

> *"I didn't run from you. All I saw were two headlights coming at me. I waited for you to go by, and I left! When you turned on the gumball, I pulled over immediately!"*

> *"Give me your license!"*

I complied. The officer ordered me to follow him back down to the "scene of the crime". When we were back at the bottom of the ski slope, the officer got out of his car, pulled out his flashlight, and started searching the side of the road, for evidence. A couple of minutes, he came back to the car with several beer bottles, with foam still in them.

> *"Tell me these aren't yours!"*

> *"They're not mine!"*

> *"Oh yeah? Well, what were you doing down here?"*

I racked my brain for an answer, and spurted out the first thing that came to mind:

> *"Parking!"*

> "Parking??? One girl and four guys?"

> "I didn't mean that kind of parking."

My mind just kicked into overdrive, and I weaved one hell of a lie:

> "We were heading up to the Teen Center. I had never been there before, and too a wrong turn, and ended up down here. When I realized that I was in the wrong place, I tried to turn the car around, but stalled the engine. Since my battery is weak, I turned off the lights, so that I didn't drain the power. That's when you came upon us. I got the car started, turned on the headlights, and started to drive out the way I came in, but you were heading straight for us. We had no idea who you were!"

The officer's face tensed up, out of sheer frustration. He didn't know whether to shit or wind his watch. He handed me back my license, and continued to admonish me:

> *"Get back into your car, start it up, and get the hell out of here. And, if I ever catch you down here at night again, I'm going to arrest you!"*

I didn't argue on what grounds he would arrest me. I bit my tongue, got back in the car, and drove away. We all let out a huge sigh of relief. Nothing was said for several seconds, as I drove toward the Teen Center. Then, David broke the silence from the back seat:

> *"That was the coolest thing I've ever seen!"*

> *"Shut the F--- up, David!"*

Chapter Twenty-Nine
Underaged Partying

Yeah, we "partied". In retrospect, we were lucky. Nobody died, nobody got arrested. That didn't make it any less irresponsible.

Typically, we would find someone to buy liquor for us, if not buy it ourselves. I actually was able to buy at the local package store when I was about sixteen. I guess I looked older.

Although I'm sure that there were others, one incident stands out, for me. One winter, I had found a gallon of apple cider in our basement that Dad had stored there. It had gone hard. Well, having heard all the stories about "Hard Cider", I stole it, to provide the evening's entertainment. I brought it over to Karl's house, and we took off to drink our fill.

Well, it worked, and we were pretty loopy. No problem, whatsoever; until I went home, and tried to go to sleep. That's when I started suffering a severe case of "Bed Spin". I then felt all that cider working its way back up. Fortunately, I normally slept with my window open, even in winter. I crawled to the end of my bed, opened the storm window, stuck my head out, and barfed down the side of the house.

All of a sudden, the storm window came down, right on my neck, and locked. I fumbled at the latches, trying to free myself from my predicament, but was too messed up to succeed. I finally gave up, and passed out with my head exposed to the elements.

When I finally awoke, it was morning. It was cold, and there was a layer of freshly fallen snow on the ground. The problem was, I couldn't open my left eye. I reached my hand out the window to assess the problem, and felt a mound of snow had formed on the left side of my face. When I finally escaped from my temporary restraint, and pulled myself back into the warmth of my room, it took a half hour to finally thaw out.

I then got dressed went outside, and used the garden hose to wash the frozen spaghetti off of the side of the house.

Chapter Thirty
Loose Girls

There comes a time, for every teenaged boy, that Playboys, National Geographics, or your mom's Cosmopolitan magazine didn't do it for you, anymore. With hormones raging, you seek out the "real thing" – something you didn't have to hold up with one hand.

There were three kinds of girls, when I was growing up – the kind of girl you take home to mom, the loose girl, and the girl you <u>wish</u> was loose, who didn't know you were alive.

We had our share of "loose girls" in our town. Loose, to us, meant that the girl would let you feel her up. It rarely ever meant intercourse. That is, until the "Looney" sisters moved into our neighborhood. There were three of them – Carrie (17), Bonnie (14) and Margie (13) – and they were the "first" for many of the guys in and around our neighborhood. Truth be told, they would bang anyone, and did.

I used to deliver newspapers to their house, and one afternoon, while dropping their paper in their porch mailbox, I looked in their living room window, and there was David Corrado, lying on the living room floor, getting cozy with Carrie. This was too good to pass up. I quietly snuck in the front door, and tiptoed to the living room and, in my most adult tone, yelled *"What the HELL is going on here???"*

I don't recall David's feet ever hitting the floor. I just remember him flying out the back door, like he was fired out of a cannon, while trying to zip up his pants. When he finally realized it was me, I think that, if he thought he could get away with it, my photo would have ended up on a milk carton.

One time, the sisters decided to do the entire high school baseball team. They formed a line down the stairs and out the front door. The only problem – their mom came home early. Boys were running out of every door and flying out of open windows, with their clothes in hand, with Mom chasing after them, and screaming at the top of her lungs.

It was shortly thereafter that the sisters and their family packed up and moved away, forever taking their place in the annals of Delmont Street lore.

Chapter Thirty-One
Saying Goodbye to "The Gang"

Kids grow up, make new friends, attain new interests, drift apart.

I mentioned earlier that music has played a huge part in my life. I started playing the drums in garage bands at the age of twelve, one band after another, none of them very good. I would sit in the background, pounding on the pagan skins, while a series of off-key lead singers would bore the audience to death. One band would break up, and another one would start – none of them very successful.

Then, something would happen to me that would change my whole life. It was 1974 – two weeks into summer vacation. Ted had moved out of the neighborhood earlier that year, and Karl and I were riding our "ten-speeds" over to Ted's new house to go swimming, one evening. We were on Henry Street, right next to Bowers Elementary School, when my foot slipped off of my bike pedal, and went directly into the spokes. I flipped head-first over the handlebars, and landed directly on my right shoulder, separating it in three places. Karl ran to a neighbor's house, and called my dad, who took me to the hospital.

I was put into traction, and told that I would be very lucky if I ever got full mobility in my arm. The doctor told there would be no more football, probably no more baseball, and I would be "strapped up" for the entire summer. I was looking at a long recovery process. Drums were out, too. If I couldn't use my arm, I couldn't play. I was miserable.

That first day home, I laid in bed, feeling sorry for myself. Ted and Karl eventually came over to see me. They walked in my bedroom, saw me lying there, obviously in great pain, and laughed their freakin' asses off! What pals!

With about a week left of summer vacation, I was allowed to remove the shoulder harness, and resume a normal life. It rained all week.

School started – my senior year. I wanted to make this _my_ year. As I had done all through school, I was involved in the choir, both during and after school, in the form of The Roundtable Singers, which was a hand-picked chorus, by Miss White, the choir teacher. She also produced the annual talent show, which was being cast in October. I wanted to be in the show, but, to do what? Well, American Graffiti had been released, Happy Days had just started on television, and fifties music was reborn. On the last day of auditions, I recruited Jon Adams, Neil Snuffer and Brian Beggs from the Roundtable to sing with me, along with Terry Sullivan on piano. We went into a practice room, and rehearsed Come Go With Me, by the Del Vikings. We passed the tryout. We then recruited Mitch Dul, from the MHS Jazz Band to play sax with us.

On Friday, November 2, 1974, The Nifty Fifty Boys made their first public appearance, at the high school talent show. We were the last act of the evening. We came blasting into the auditorium from one of the exit doors, and the audience exploded. We opened with Silhouettes by the Rays, followed by Come Go with Me. Standing ovation!

It all changed that night. We turned this little talent show act into a full-fledged band, changed the name to The Nifty Fifties Band, and set out to conquer the New England concert scene. Gigs started piling up, and we found ourselves spending every free moment rehearsing for, traveling to, or performing a gig.

It was hard enough that Larry had graduated the year before me, David the year after, Karl the year after David, while Ted was working all the time. But, this new opportunity really took us apart. As time went by, we saw less and less of each other. Between my band, their jobs, school, and our girlfriends, we saw less and less of each other. Unless they came to see my band play, I never saw them. We ran in different circles, now. Sure, we got together on occasion, but things were changing, and we knew it. We were growing up; we were finding a world outside of Delmont Street.

There's something sad about the fact that we had to grow up. Would anything ever be as fun as when you hung around with your friends from the old neighborhood? I don't think so.

I will never forget those guys. We don't get the chance to see each other very often, but when any of us get together, we still have a good time, and we still laugh. But, it's not the same unbridled madness as it was when we were kids, driving our parents crazy. It can't be;

because now <u>we're</u> the parents, and we have to be respectable, upstanding pillars of society. And, what fun is that?

We were friends, we were adversaries; we were the Delmont Street Gang. At least, that's what we wanted to believe.

Chapter Thirty-Two
Where Are They Now?

Larry Smith is a project manager for a general contractor. He has been married for years to Sharon.

Karl Smith is an Account Analysis Director for a marketing firm. He is married to Jane, and has two kids.

Reese Smith is a software engineer for a national insurance company. He is married to Donna, and has two sons.

David Corrado is a general contractor and restaurant owner. He is married, and has a son, named "Little David".

"Doctor Bob" Corrado, David's dad, is still kicking, at 89 years of age. I sent him some chapters of this book, and he laughed like hell.

Matt Haley is a long-time distributor for a beer company, and still funny as hell.

Ryan Haley is professionally unemployed.

Ken Hanson is a partner in an insurance firm. He is married with two kids.

Craig Haley died on January 9, 2002, of colon cancer. He was cremated and, to this day, family and friends take his ashes with them, whenever they go on vacation, to spread the word about this preventable disease. "Here's Craig, at the Grand Canyon", or "Here's Craig at Fenway Park"... You get the picture.

George Hanson died way too young, of complications from lymphoma. He was 31, and a real good guy.

Ted Hanson is manager of national-chain flooring store. He is divorced, with two kids – Sherry and Theodore Joseph. He's a great dad.

My mom died in 2003. She was 79. I miss her. I miss our talks.

My dad was dying, in Pennsylvania. I took the "red eye" to Baltimore, and drove straight to the hospital, in York, PA.

When I walked into Dad's room, my sisters, and their families, were there. Jessica (older sister) said *"Dad,*

Eric's here."

"Eric? Where's Eric?"

"Right here, Pop. How are ya feelin'?"

(smiles) "Eh, not bad."

He was old, frail and all but blind. But, he still kept his sense of humor. We talked, I told him the "Joke of the Day", and he laughed.

Soon, the hospital grief counselor brought my sisters and I into the hallway, to prepare us for the inevitable. She gave us a pamphlet, which I affectionately called "The Book of Death". Essentially, it explained the different stages of death, and what to expect. It was meant to ease us into the transition.

A section of the book talked about "The Rally", which is the final stage before death, where the patient has one last burst of energy, like the last squeeze on a tube of toothpaste. Many times, the patient will become lucid and start talking. Then, shortly thereafter, it's over.

After several hours of waiting, I was exhausted, and needed to sleep. I excused myself, and drove to Dad's house, for the night.

The following morning, my cell phone rang. It was Jessica. *"Dad's rallying, and he's talking up a storm. You had better get here, quick!"* I quickly drove to the hospital.

Dad was talking to everyone on "the other side" – Mom, his parents, his in-laws, and his brothers. Now, the strangest part of this was that several months before, our Aunt Gerry, Dad's brother's wife, had died. We never told Dad about it, as we didn't think he needed to be upset unnecessarily. Anyway, all of a sudden, Dad exclaims: *"Gerry! What the heck are YOU doing here?? I didn't know you died!"*

Jessy asked him if he was going to Heaven. He told us he was. Jessy asked him if he wanted to say his prayers. He replied: *"What for? I'm already here!"*

Dad died the next day, June 12, 2006, with a smile on

his face. Dignity in life – dignity in death. He will always be my hero.

I live in Las Vegas, with my high school sweetheart, Sue and our son, Nick, We have a grandson, named Nathan, who loves his Mama and Papa, and brings us great joy. I work at a local firm, and delude myself that I'm an author, in my spare time.

Ted came out to Las Vegas for a visit, a short time ago. While he was here, I brought him to a friend's birthday party, thinking he'd get a big kick out of meeting some of my Vegas friends. The only problem was, we showed up for the party ON THE WRONG NIGHT! Ted laughed his ass off:

"Ahhh hah hah hahhhh! SHIT ON! Nice going, assface! You just pulled a Mann!"

(Sigh!) Some things never change!

Chapter Thirty-Three
Bonus Stories

I may not ever get another chance to write these stories down so, even though they have nothing to do with the gang, I wanted to share them, with you.

My grandmother (Mom's mom) was named Alma. She grew up in Kansas, with her parents and her brother, Thomas. It was early Christmas morning – around three o'clock, to be exact – when Alma and Tom's curiosity got the best of them, and they snuck downstairs to the living room, to see what Santa had brought them.

There, under the tree, were identical Flexible Flyer snow sleds. Well, this sneaky brother and sister team couldn't contain their excitement, and decided that they would go across the street to the park, and try out their new sleds. They quietly got dressed, put on their winter gear, and gingerly snuck out of the house, to have a little forbidden fun.

After a while, Alma and Tom headed back to the house, carefully wiped down the sleds, placed them back under the tree, and snuck back to bed. Boy, they thought they were slick, having pulled off this grand deception, without a hitch.

Several hours later, it was time to get up to join mom and dad, to officially start the Christmas festivities. When Tom and Alma returned to the living room and looked under the tree, the sleds were gone! They looked at each other in astonishment. Where could they have gone??? Did mom and dad find out? Or, was it a power greater than them? Did Santa exact a little revenge?

They would never know. For they were smart enough to realize that they could never ask their parents about the whereabouts of their prized sleds; that would mean that they had seen them already, and they would have some serious explaining to do. Nope! They decided that they would have to keep their mouths shut – forever!

Years passed, and the sleds were never discussed. In fact, Alma and Tom's parents went to their graves without ever hearing the truth from their children. And, throughout their entire lives, Alma and Tom never found out where the sleds went.

Years later, Alma would marry Herman Meyer (my granddad), and give birth to Marilyn (My mom), Wayne

(My uncle), and Adele (My aunt), and raise her family in Kansas City, Kansas.

As was the norm during the thirties, grocery stores routinely ran sales promotions to boost business. One time, they held a contest in which the person who bought the most rolls of Scott's Toilet Paper would win a beautiful 28-inch boys bicycle. Well, Alma decided that she just had to win this bike for her precious son, Wayne. So, she proceeded to call Mr. Martin, the grocer, and order two full cartons of toilet paper to be delivered to her house. They were quickly delivered, and stored in Alma's basement.

Mrs. Freeman, another customer of Carter's market, who had decided that she was going to win the grand prize for her son, got a call from Mr. Carter, who informed her that Mrs. Meyer had just bought two cartons of toilet paper. Well, not wanting to be outdone, Mrs. Freeman requested three cartons to be delivered to her house.

Mr. Carter knew when he had a good thing going, and called Alma, to squeal on the competition. Alma ordered two more! This went on for a few days, until Mrs.

Freeman finally threw in the towel. Alma had won the bicycle! Victory was hers!! She had a basement full of toilet paper, but the better person had won!

Over the next several years, whenever there was a birthday, or anniversary, or a house warming party, the guest of honor would receive a carton of <u>Scott's Toilet Paper</u>, with a huge bow on it, courtesy of my future grandmother, Alma Meyer.

Wayne never rode the bike – not once.

As I had said before, Mom and Dad met and started dating while attending DePaul University, in Chicago. One day, while leaving the CTA line (elevated train), and walking down the stairs to the street, Mom lost her footing and took a slight fall. Mom always carried a large purse, more along the lines of a carpet bag. This day was no exception.

Everything flew out of Mom's bag and landed everywhere. Mom and Dad scurried to pick up the contents of mom's huge purse, when an unfamiliar voice was heard, saying *"Madam, I believe this is yours."* Mom and Dad looked up to see an older, well-dressed gentleman, wearing a neatly creased fedora hat, with one of mom's Kotex pads lying in the crease of his hat, the string dangling in the poor man's face.

I'm told that this was cause for one of the longest sustained laughs my parents and the gentleman would ever experience.

Then, there was the time after Mom and Dad were married, that they were passengers on an ocean liner, on their way to Australia. Back then, everyone dressed appropriately for dinner, in their finest outfits. Mom and Dad were invited to dine at the captain's table, with assorted VIP's joining them. There was a sumptuous meal, dancing, and a lot of champagne. Although my parents were never big drinkers, I guess the festive atmosphere got the best of Mom, and she ended up getting a bit "tipsy".

Feeling a bit overheated, she asked the other guests: *"Is it me, or is it hot in here?"*

As was the custom for ladies back then, she reached into the neckline of her dress to retrieve her handkerchief, and pulled it out to begin dabbing at her face. The other guests at the table were starting to laugh uncontrollably, when my mom say the look of horror on

Dad's face. She looked down to see that instead of her handkerchief, she was holding her bra in her hand.

Needless to say, I don't think they were invited back to the captain's table.

Now, It's Your Turn!

Do you have a story to share from your childhood? I need material for another book, and thought that there must be thousands of "nuggets" out there. Send me your stories to ericmann702@gmail.com. Please include your contact information, so that I can get in touch with you.

If your story is published, you will get full credit and, who knows, I may even send you a couple of bucks!

Thanks for reading!

Made in the USA
Lexington, KY
27 November 2017